NOTES ON THE FIRST EPISTLE TO THE CORINTHIANS

JOHN MILLER

Copyright © Hayes Press 2018

All rights reserved. No part of this book may be reproduced, stored in a retrieval system, or transmitted in any form, without the written permission of Hayes Press.

Published by:

HAYES PRESS

The Barn, Flaxlands

Royal Wootton Bassett

Swindon, SN4 8DY

United Kingdom

www.hayespress.org

Unless otherwise indicated, all Scripture quotations are from the Revised Version, 1885 (RV, Public Domain). Scriptures marked KJV are from the King James Version, 1611 (Public Domain).

INTRODUCTION: PAUL'S LETTERS TO THE CORINTHIANS - WHEN AND WHERE WRITTEN (W. BUNTING)

Two incidents stand out as reasons for the apostle Paul writing his first epistle to the church of God in Corinth. He had heard from the household of Chloe the disturbing news that contentions had arisen in the church, and that the saints were taking sides, saying, "I am of Paul; and I of Apollos; and I of Cephas; and I of Christ" (1 Cor.1:11,12). The second reason was the receipt of a letter from Corinth raising important questions regarding marital relationships (1 Cor.7:1). In his epistle, Paul deals with these two matters, and much else besides.

That the epistle was written from Ephesus seems to be borne out by the statement, "I will tarry at Ephesus until Pentecost" (1 Cor.16:8). He had previously disclosed his plans to go to Corinth through Macedonia, and he hoped even to winter there (1 Cor.16:5,6). It is evident that Apollos was with the apostle in Ephesus at the time of writing this letter (1 Cor.16:12). We know from Acts 18:27 that some time later Apollos visited Achaia, and helped the saints there and confuted the Jews. The epistle must have been written towards the end of Paul's long stay in Ephesus. Aquila and Prisca were still with him in that city, and sent their salutation to Corinth, where they must have been well known. In addition, the churches of Asia joined in the salutations (1 Cor.16:19).

After the uproar in Ephesus instigated by Demetrius the silversmith, the apostle took leave of the Ephesian saints, and departed to go into Macedonia (Acts 20:1). On the way he stopped at Troas, where the Lord opened a door unto him. However, he was very disappointed at not finding Titus there. "I had no relief for my spirit, because I found not Titus my brother: but taking my leave of them, I went forth into Macedonia" (2 Cor. 2:13). Even in Macedonia the apostle had no relief, and he speaks of fightings without, and fears within. The situation is changed by the arrival of Titus, who had come from Corinth, and brought comforting news of the saints in that city, and reported their zeal for the apostle. Titus also informed Paul of the results of his first epistle to the Corinthians (2 Cor.7:5-16). It seems that upon receipt of this information, the apostle wrote his second epistle to the church in Corinth. If this be so, it was written in Macedonia. It contains some very passionate passages, and also conveys deep, spiritual truths. In addition, some remarkable experiences are recorded of the apostle's sufferings in the service of Christ.

COMMENTARY ON 1 CORINTHIANS 1

1 Cor.1:1,2,3

Paul was a called apostle or an apostle by calling; his call to apostleship was to become his vocation in life. This call was through the will of God. He associates Sosthenes with himself in the writing of this epistle. Sosthenes was a Jew, the ruler of the synagogue who lived in Corinth, and who, no doubt, was converted under the apostle's ministry (Acts 18:17). He calls Sosthenes "the" brother. Those to whom the epistle was written are described as "the church of God which is at (En in) Corinth." "Church" is the English translation of the Greek word ekklesia, which is derived from ek, out of, and kaleo, to call, and means a called-out people. The word "church" is not used in both singular and plural in any other application of the word in the New Testament, save in the case of the church of God and the churches of God.

The word in the original, usually rendered "church," is used in a secular sense in Acts 19:32,39, where it is translated "assembly." It is used of Israel, the church in the wilderness (Acts 7:38). It is also used of the Church which is His (Christ's) Body, which comprises all saved people of this dispensation from Pentecost until the Lord's coming again (Eph.1:22,23; Eph.5:25-27). It is also used of that company of heavenly beings called "the church of the firstborn (ones) who are enrolled in heaven" (Heb.12:23). It also defines the house of God as "the church of the living God" (1 Tim.3:15). These uses are all in the singular. Then we have "the churches of Christ" and "the churches of the saints" (Rom.16:16; 1 Cor.14:33). We do not read of the church of Christ or the church of the saints in the New Testament. What is a church of God? It is a called-out company of God's saints in any place to carry out the will of God collectively, for the will of God cannot be done by isolated children of God.

There were many churches of God in the time of the apostles, as we see from 1 Cor.4:17; 11:16; Gal.1:2,22; 1 Thess.2:14; 2 Thess.1:4 etc. In contrast to this the Church which is His (Christ's) Body is ever one (Rom.12:5; 1 Cor.12:13; Eph.2:16, 4:4). Those who composed the church of God in Corinth were persons who were sanctified (or set apart) in Christ Jesus. Christ Jesus was their sanctification (1:30), as He was also their righteousness and redemption. No unsaved person is contemplated as being in a church of God, though, alas, at later times such as are called grievous wolves (Acts 20:29) gained an entrance by stealth (Jud.4); they crept in privily with dire results to the flock. Those who were sanctified in Christ Jesus were called saints, as the apostle was a called apostle. They had responded to the call of God in the gospel and thus were saints by calling.

They were not saints because they lived saintly lives, but those who are saints should live saintly lives, that is their vocation or calling. A mixed communion of saints and sinners is not contemplated in the New Testament. The church of God in Corinth was with (Sun, together with) all who called on the name of the Lord Jesus Christ who were gathered similarly in the churches of God in every place. The reading should be "their place and ours," though applied to the Lord, in both the AV/KJV and RV The salutation of grace and peace is common to Paul's epistles.

1 Cor.1:4,5,6

The church of God in Corinth was a highly gifted Church. They had received an abundance of grace in Christ Jesus (Eph.4:7), and were enriched in all utterance (Logos, word, discourse); they were able to express themselves well. They were also enriched in all knowledge. If their other qualities had been in similar measure to their knowledge and ability to discourse, then all would have been well. In them the testimony of Christ was established, was constant and unwavering.

1 Cor.1:7,8

Thus by being enriched through divine grace in utterance and knowledge, they came behind in no gift. This is indeed a high commendation by the apostle. They were waiting for the revelation of the Lord. This is His revelation to His saints, not His Rev.in flaming fire, as in 2 Thess.1:7,8, when He comes as Son of Man in judgement. Various words are used concerning the Lord's coming for His saints of this dispensation of grace. Gk. parousia, which means "presence," is usually translated "coming." It is derived from para, near or beside, and eimi, I am. It is of frequent use concerning the Lord's coming. It is also used of the coming of the Lord as the Son of Man to earth (Matt.24:3,27,37,39). Gk. erchomai, which means to travel, is used in Jn 14:3 of the Lord's coming again.

Whilst erchomai means to travel, parousia, in contrast, signifies arrival. Erchomai is also used of the coming of the Son of Man (Matt.24:30). Gk. epiphaino, to appear, from epi, upon, and phaino, to shine, is used of the appearing of the saving grace of God at the Lord's first coming (Tit.2:11). It is also used, in Tit.2:13, of the appearing of the glory of our great God and Saviour, Jesus Christ, the blessed hope of believers. Gk. phaneroo, to manifest, from phaino, to shine, is used of the Lord in His first coming to put away sins (1 Jn 3:5; Heb.9:26), and also to destroy the works of the devil (1 Jn 3:8). It is also used of His coming again for His saints (1 Jn 2:28; 3:2; 1 Pet.5:4). Gk. optomai, to see, to behold with the eyes (Heb.9:28), is used of the Lord appearing to His waiting saints, as did the high priest of old when he emerged from the sanctuary to the waiting people outside.

Gk apokalupsis, an uncovering, rendered "revelation," that is, His Rev.to His saints, as in 1 Cor.1:7; 1 Pet.1:7,13; 4:13: It is also used of the Rev.of the Son of Man (2 Thess.1:7), and in its verbal form (Gk. apokalupto, to reveal) of the revealing of the Son of Man (Lk.17:30), when every eye shall see Him. The expectation of saints is expressed in different words; Gk. anameno, to wait (1 Thess.1:10). Gk. prosdechomai, to look, to expect (Tit.2:13). Gk. apekdechomai, to expect, to wait for with the object of receiving (1 Cor.1:7; Phil.3:20; Heb.9:28). The coming again of our Lord is a matter of supreme importance for us and should be one of great expectancy. What day is the day of the Lord Jesus Christ? In 1 Cor.5:5 Paul speaks of the day of the Lord Jesus (rendered by some as the day of the Lord Jesus Christ). I take it that what Paul had in view was the saving of the spirit of the sinning brother in the then present day, the day of grace. He was delivered unto Satan for the destruction of the flesh that his spirit might be saved, and this was effected, as we know from 2 Cor.2:5-11.

The church in Corinth was told to commend their love to him in his sorrow for his past act. I therefore think what the apostle writes of, in 1 Cor.1:8, was that the saints should be unreprovable or unimpeachable in the then present day, in this day of grace, not in the day of the Lord's coming. That day is the day of Christ (Phil.1:10). Note the difference, "in (En) the day of our Lord Jesus Christ, "but "unto the day of Christ," or "until the day of Jesus Christ" (Phil.1:6).

1 Cor.1:9

The Greek word for fellowship is koinonia, derived from koinos, common. It has various meanings, or shades of meaning. It may mean, according to the context, community, communion, society, fellowship, partnership, participation. The use of the word in the above verse is that of a community of people. It is similar in meaning to its use in Acts 2:42, where those who had been saved, baptized and added, continued stedfastly in the apostles' teaching, in the Fellowship, and in the breaking of the bread, and in the prayers. Fellowship in 1 Jn 1 is communion.

First the communion of the apostles was with the Father and the Son; then that communion broadened to communion between the apostles and the saints, and then between the saints. This communion is possible where saints walk in the light, and where there is confession of sin and conformity to God's word, then this sweet experience of communion may be known.

There was one Fellowship or Community in the apostles' days into which the saints in the churches of God were called, and therein as a sacred and common trust they held, and continued in, the apostles' teaching. This was a prime function of their being together. Where need of a material kind arose, then they were responsible to have fellowship with the needy. See the use of the word koinonia, fellowship, in Rom.15, where we read of the churches of God in the provinces of Macedonia and Achaia sending by the apostle and others a contribution (fellowship) to the poor in Jerusalem. Their act showed how truly they were in the same Fellowship or Community (Rom.15,26; 1 Cor.16:1-9; and 2 Cor.8 and 9).

1 Cor.1:10

Gk. parakaleo is sometimes rendered "beseech" and sometimes "exhort." Paul beseeches them, not on the ground of his labours among them, but in the name of the Lord Jesus Christ, to whom they were indebted for so very much. His object in this was that they would all speak the same thing, and that they would be free from divisions (Gk. schismata, rents, ruptures. See Matt.9:16; Mk.2:21, where schisma is rendered rent). In contrast, Paul wishes them to be perfected together or knit together (Gk. katartizo, to repair or mend; this was what James and John, the sons of Zebedee, were doing when the Lord called them; they were mending their nets). The Corinthians were to be knit together in the same mind and in the same judgement. (Judgement, Gk. gnome, means mode of thinking. The word is derived from ginosko, to learn, to acquire knowledge.) As a result of having learned, they could think together in a similar mode of thinking and in consequence reach a sameness of judgement or decision.

1 Cor.1:11,12

It had been signified (Gk. deloo, to lay open) by those of Chloe (the word household is not in the passage, though it may be implied) that contentions (Gk. eris, strife, contention) existed among the Corinthians. This Christian woman, Chloe, is nowhere else mentioned in the New Testament. Those of Chloe were no doubt in the church in Corinth, whether they were children or servants is unknown. Each one was preferring one servant of Christ above another, and in this internecine strife the Lord was being preferred above Paul, as though He were to be regarded as a servant among the rest, instead of being the Lord over all. It may be that Paul uses these names figuratively in order to teach them not to be puffed up among themselves for the one against the other. See what is said in 1 Cor.4:6: Note also what is said in 3:4-8: It may however be, in the verse above, that they were preferring those whose names are mentioned the one above the other, and that 1 Cor.4:6 is to be linked with 1 Cor.3:4-8: Whichever be the correct view of these passages, it is evident that the contentions were grievous and serious and could, if unchecked, only lead to partyism or sectarianism in the church and completely destroy that unity which was of God.

1 Cor.1:13,14,15,16,17

"Is Christ divided?" (Merizo, to divide or disunite by discord). In the strife that existed it would appear as though He had been divided into parts. Had Paul been crucified (Aorist tense, was this an historical fact?) for them? Had they been baptized (Aorist tense, was this also an historical fact?) into the name of Paul? The answer in each case was, No. He thanked God that he had baptized none, save Crispus and Gaius and the household of Stephanas. (See 1 Cor.16:15; this man and his household were the firstfruits of Achaia, and they were all grown-up persons, for they set themselves to minister to the saints. They were baptized that they might baptize others). Paul gives the reason why it was not his custom to baptize disciples which he made, lest it should be said that they were baptized into the name of Paul. He was sent to preach the gospel by the Lord, not to baptize. This must not be taken as signifying that baptism is of little importance. It is a command of the Lord, and none of His commandments are unimportant.

As was the household of Stephanas, so was the Jailor's household in Acts 16:31-34: "And they said, Believe on the Lord Jesus, and thou shalt be saved, thou and thy house. And he took them the same hour of the night, and washed their stripes; and was baptized, he and all his, immediately ... and rejoiced greatly, with all his house, having believed in God." There was no little child or unsaved person in the Jailor's household who was baptized. The same is true of the household of Lydia the purple-seller (Acts 16:14,15). The same is also true of Cornelius and his household (Acts 10:1,2,33,44- 48). Those of the household of Cornelius all believed and the Holy Spirit fell upon them, and afterwards they were baptized at the command of Peter.

The cross of Christ is the great leveller. It gives to man not a footbreadth of his own merit to stand upon. Mankind is segregated into all kinds of systems, parties, sects and schisms. After man is humbled in the dust before the cross and knows the Lord as his Saviour, then baptism into the name of the Trinity, Father, Son and Holy Spirit (Matt.28:19,20), should follow, and disciples should be taught to observe all the things which the Lord commanded. Alas, how soon after conversion believers drift into sects and parties in Christendom and are found gathered under names which find no place in the Scriptures; thus the cross of Christ is made void!

1 Cor.1:18,19

Paul has two classes before his mind, the perishing ones and the saved ones, sinners and saints, not saints who are losing their lives, and saints whose lives are being saved. To the perishing the word of the cross is foolishness, but to those who are being saved it is the power of God. The scene of what seemed defeat was the scene of the greatest victory. Here the world was overcome, the flesh crucified, sin put away, and the devil defeated, and here should end too sects and schisms, the result of the will of the flesh. God has by the cross destroyed the wisdom of the wise, and rejected the understanding of the understanding ones. Here human philosophy met its death, for what man counts wisdom God counts foolishness, and what God counts wisdom man counts foolishness. There can be no reconciliation of the two points of view. Who is right? The answer is obvious. Christ crucified is God's wisdom for men. It is the great unifier of men. See Jn 11:51,52: on the ground of His death saints are to be gathered together, and Israel will yet be gathered one by one (Isa.27:12), for the Lord died for that nation, and it will become the centre of government and worship in millennial days.

1 Cor.1:20,21

As the wisdom of God and the wisdom of the world met in a head-on collision at the cross with the destruction of the latter, which will in due time be fully seen, God challenges the wise, and says, "Where is the wise?" Where was the Jewish scribe and the Gentile disputer of the age? Paul disputed with all classes as to the cross, in Jewish synagogues and with the Greek philosophers on Mars Hill in Athens. All systems of human thought are doomed; only that will stand which originated in the divine mind. The cross stands as God's answer to human need in all its phases, and man's first need is that of wisdom, and Christ crucified is God's wisdom. "In the wisdom of God the world through its wisdom knew not God." If man clings to his own wisdom he will never know God's. Let human wisdom be heaped up mountains high, man at the top will be no nearer knowing God than he who is at the bottom. Only through the cross is God fully revealed to men. Of old the question was asked, "Canst thou by searching find out God?" (Job 11:7). God is to be known by revelation, not by investigation. God has revealed Himself in Christ crucified. It was God's good pleasure (Aorist tense, an historical fact) through the foolishness (that is, foolishness as the world counts foolishness) of what is preached, even the cross of Christ, to save the believing ones.

1 Cor.1:22,23,24,25

"Jews ask for signs"; these were frequently asked for during the Lord's ministry: "Master, we would see a sign from Thee" (Matt.12:38: See also Matt.16:1; Lk.11:16; Lk.23:8; Jn 2:18, etc.), but the Greeks sought wisdom. Amongst them were the philosophers, the lovers of wisdom. Christ crucified, a Man who died under the curse of hanging upon a tree, was to the unenlightened Jew a stumbling-block, and to the Gentiles this Man who died as a common criminal under Roman law was foolishness. But to the called, that is, those who heard the call of God and responded to it, whether Jews or Greeks, and in consequence were saved, Christ was both the power of God, and the wisdom of God. He, the wisdom of God, who was in the place of the skull, gives wisdom to such as have none of their own.

It seems strange to speak of the foolishness of God and the weakness of God, but we understand this of Him who is God and Man, one Christ, who was crucified through weakness (2 Cor.13:4), yet in His weakness is stronger than all human strength combined, and wiser than all human wisdom. Human wisdom lauded in one generation is often discarded by the following generations, but Christ crucified will remain. "Our little systems have their day, They have their day and cease to be." That wisdom in Corinth which contended, "I am of Paul," "I am of Apollos," has long since perished, gone as sand-castles on the shore before the in-rolling tide. The arm of man falls powerless, the mind of man becomes worn out and decayed, but the word of the cross remains from age to age imperishable.

1 Cor.1:26

This call is not that of 2 Cor.6:14-18, in which those who were saved were called to a path of separation, called out to do God's will, and called into the Fellowship of His Son Jesus Christ our Lord (1:9), which Fellowship was expressed in the church of God in Corinth and in the churches of God elsewhere. The call in the above verse is what we may call the gospel call, as is indicated in Rom.8:30, "Whom He foreordained, them He also called: and whom He called, them He also justified: and whom He justified, them He also glorified." See also 2 Thess.2:13,14, etc. No sinner is called out of any association or so-called church before he can be saved. God saves sinners where they are. The whole world system and associations of men are wrong in His sight.

Some associations of men are confessedly worse than others, but all are wrong. The gospel call is that men should everywhere come to Christ for salvation, and only after that does God call upon them to come out from those and from that with which they have been previously associated. Often that call is refused by believers. Not many wise after the flesh are called, that is, called with what has been called "effectual calling," the call heard and responded to. In another sense, "Many called, but few chosen" (Matt.22:14). Many, alas, have heard the call and rejected it to their eternal condemnation. Not many mighty, not many noble or high-born are called. It has been said that "the ancient Christians were for the most part slaves and men of low station."

1 Cor.1:27,28,29

The effectual calling of God rests upon the choosing of God, the two cannot be disunited. Such matters are beyond our powers of reasoning, and we cannot charge God with injustice or bias. God's actions have in view that He will not tolerate flesh, that is, mankind, to glory before Him. The proud He will not endure. Hence, He chose deliberately the foolish, the weak, the low-born and despised, in contrast to the wise, strong, and high-born, though not altogether, for a few high-born, wise and strong, are found among His chosen. So, as James says, "Let the brother of low degree glory in his high estate: and the rich, in that he is made low" (Jas.1:9,10). God even chooses things that do not exist as yet, that he might annul the things that do exist. How strange are the ways of God, they are past finding out (Rom.11:33)! There will be no boasting of personal merit among all the hosts of the redeemed, and there is no pandering to human pride by God.

1 Cor.1:30,31

The work of God leaves no place for human boasting, for "of Him are ye in Christ Jesus." God is the Source of all good giving and good doing, and besides Him there is none good. We are not simply made wise in Christ Jesus (4:10), but He is our wisdom. We must not think to mingle our wisdom with His, such as we think we have. He is the wisdom of saints in totality, for they have none of their own. He is also our righteousness, for we had none. He is both our Sanctifier and our sanctification, for we were unholy. He is also our Redeemer and our redemption. He is Jehovah-tsidkenu (Heb.), "the LORD is our righteousness" (Jer.23:6: Jer.33:16). He is Jehovah-mekadishim (Heb.), "I am the LORD which sanctify you" (Ex.31:13). He is Jehovah my Goel (Heb.), "the LORD ... my Redeemer" (Ps.19:14).

COMMENTARY ON 1 CORINTHIANS 2

1 Cor.2:1,2

As Paul left philosophic and sinful Athens behind, and came to the sinful commercial city of Corinth, he came not with the polish or rhetoric of a philosopher. None of the arts of oratory used by the Greeks was used by him. His decision in proclaiming the mystery (some say testimony) of God, which is Christ (Col.2:2), was not to know (Gk. oida, what he saw by revelation, not what he had learned) anything, save Jesus Christ, and Him crucified. Christ crucified is the sole and only message which God has for sinful men. There is no other remedy for sin. Many cures have been tried, but they have left the filthiness of the human heart untouched. Human wisdom and human sin flow in the same stream. The heart must be cleansed by an efficient cleanser, even the blood of Jesus God's Son, or man will remain a sinner. Hence Paul's decision as to his message in Corinth.

1 Cor.2:3,4,5

Here Paul reveals his state of mind in his early days in Corinth. He was in weakness and fear and in much trembling. There was no self-confidence in him, but utter dependence upon God and the power of his message, which is the power of God unto salvation to the believer (Rom.1:16). This message came unto the Cor.in the power and demonstration of the Spirit. This was to the end that their faith, the result of the message preached, for faith cometh by hearing, and hearing by the word of Christ (Rom.10:17), might not stand in the wisdom of men, in the mere emotionalism and enthusiasm produced by oratory, but in the power of God. Faith must be (there is no word for "stand") in the word of God and not in the wisdom of man's works, if faith is to be genuine.

1 Cor.2:6

Paul's message to the world was Christ, and Him crucified. But this was not all that he had to tell. He spoke wisdom among the perfect or full-grown, that is, full-grown in mind and understanding of divine things. Yet this wisdom was not of this world (age), nor of the rulers of this world (age), for both these rulers and this wisdom are coming to nought. But, sad to say, men build their towers of human wisdom on the mouldering bones of systems which have perished.

1 Cor.2:7,8

Men and their wisdom are coming to nought, only God and His wisdom are permanent. But God's wisdom is hidden from the wise as to this world, even as the Lord said, "I thank Thee, O Father, Lord of heaven and earth, that Thou didst hide these things from the wise and understanding, and didst reveal them unto babes" (Matt.11:25). It is God's prerogative to reveal and to conceal. God's wisdom is revealed unto His saints; it was foreordained unto our glory. None of the rulers knew what the apostles, fishermen and others from Galilee, knew. Annas and Caiaphas, Pontius Pilate and Herod, and many, many others besides knew nothing of this wisdom, "for" says Paul, "had they known it, they would not have crucified the Lord of glory." Not only is this wisdom a mystery to men, but the ways of God in hiding it from men are also a mystery to us; yet in so doing there is no unrighteousness with God. God be praised that He has been pleased to reveal His secret to those who have believed!

1 Cor.2:9,10

The words of this quotation seem to be a free rendering of Isa.64:4, though some think that the words of Isa.52:15 are paraphrased by Paul. It may well be that the difficulty here, which has been seen by many in both ancient and modern times, is to be explained by the fact that

Paul gives the essential meaning of much that is written in the Old Testament, that what God has prepared for them that love Him has never entered the eye or ear or heart of man. What God has prepared of His goodness for them that love Him is made known to them by revelation. Hence between what men understand, see and hear naturally, and what God has revealed there is a chasm which cannot be crossed. Thus Paul says, "But unto us God revealed them through the Spirit: for the Spirit searcheth all things, yea, the deep things of God." How great is this wonder, that this searching and revealing Spirit has been given to each believer! that such might know what God has prepared for them. See Rev.21 and 22 as to what God has prepared for them that love the Lord.

1 Cor.2:11,12

What man is able to know (Gk. oida, to see) what is in the mind of another? Only a man's own spirit knows what is in the depths of his mind. Even so no one knoweth (Gk. egnoken, hath known; the word is a form of ginosko, to learn) the things of God except the Spirit of God. We received not the spirit of the world, which, as Eph.2:2 shows, is "the prince of the power of the air, ... the spirit that now worketh in the sons of disobedience." In contrast, we received the Spirit which is from (Gk. ek, out of) God, that we might know (Gk. oida, to see) the things that are freely given to us by God. First is given the gift of the Spirit and by Him the knowledge of what God has given to us. What grace is this!

1 Cor.2:13,14

The things which Paul and others knew by the revelation of the Spirit of God, these things they spoke in words which the Spirit also gave, not in words taught them by human wisdom. How often university-trained men conceal by their philosophies the plain meaning of Holy Scripture! Those who listen to their orations of human wisdom are either left with their minds a blank or are gratified with the wonderful extent of human wisdom. Words which the Spirit teacheth befit the things which the Spirit has revealed. The Spirit of God took Jn the Baptist into the wilderness, and Paul was taken to Arabia, two of God's great luminaries, to be taught what to say and how to say it.

Hence it follows that spiritual things are to be expounded, and hence communicated, by spiritual means, that is, by spiritual words taught by the Spirit. This is, I judge, the meaning of the original, which is rendered above as "comparing spiritual things with spiritual," words which are somewhat confusing. In contrast to this, the natural man, that is the unregenerate, soulish man, cannot receive the things of the Spirit of God. They are foolishness to him. When a spiritual address is being given or a spiritual conversation is taking place, the natural man is like a person among people of a foreign language; he knows not the meaning of what is being said. The one means of making contact with those who are spiritual is by receiving Christ crucified by faith and then the Holy Spirit is given, and by the Spirit he enters into the realm of spiritual things. But otherwise there is no means of his knowing the things of the Spirit of God.

1 Cor.2:15,16

He that is spiritual is a person indwelt by the Spirit of God, and judges things according to the mind of the Spirit, and not by natural, human reason. Such an one judges, examines or discerns, all things, but he himself cannot be judged by such as are merely natural, soulish, and consequently, unspiritual men. But how often natural men have sought to judge those that were spiritual! So dealt men of old with the prophets, and so dealt they with the Lord Himself. The apostles, prophets and saints of the New Testament have been similarly judged by natural men. What natural man has known the mind of the Lord that he should instruct the spiritual man? How many young, born-again men, have entered colleges and have been under the instruction of natural, unregenerate men, and their lives have been ruined as to their usefulness for God? Paul says that we, the spiritual, have the mind of Christ. Christ, the Servant of Jehovah, was filled with the Spirit of God from His baptism, and in the Spirit's power He wrought and taught; so believers who have the Spirit of God should be subject to His mind and so have the mind of Christ.

COMMENTARY ON 1 CORINTHIANS 3

1 Cor.3:1,2,3

We have in chapter 1 the spiritual (Gk. pneumatikos) man, the natural (Gk. psuchikos) man, and now we have the carnal (Gk. sarkikos) man. The spiritual and the carnal describe two kinds of believers, the one controlled by a spiritual mind and the other by a carnal mind. The natural man is not a believer at all, he is unregenerate. The natural man cannot receive at all the things of the Spirit of God, and the carnal believer is so weak spiritually that he must be treated as a babe and given milk, baby's food. Though the Corinthians were enriched in all knowledge and utterance, as in 1:5, yet their state was such that they had made little advancement in true Christian living. The simple elements of spiritual life were not understood and practised by them. There was among them jealousy and strife, the exact opposite of the fruit of the Spirit (Gal.5:19-23); they walked after the manner of men who have no new life and have not the Spirit, though the Corinthians had both. They evidently had clear heads, but cold hearts.

1 Cor.3:4,5,6

Here Paul returns to the contentions, born of carnality, of 1 Cor.1:11-13: Their behaviour was the behaviour of men who follow men of their choice. Oftentimes men follow men who promise them much, but give them nothing. Their promises are like the notes of a devalued currency, useless and valueless. What was Paul or Apollos? they were ministers through whom they believed, and there was no glory to the preachers, for they spoke what God gave them to speak. Converts often stick to the place where they were saved, whether it is right or wrong. In Paul's case they had a worthy example, but that was no reason why he should be preferred above another. Paul had planted the church of God in Corinth and Apollos had watered it, but their work would have been futile if God had not caused it to grow. Care should be taken between the ideas of sowing and planting. Sowing is the work of the preacher who scatters the seed of the gospel. Planting shows that the seed has germinated in human hearts, resulting in persons being viewed as plants, and these plants are taken and planted together according to the divine pattern given in the Scriptures.

What Paul refers to here about planting is one of the most ancient ideas in the Scriptures. We are told that the LORD God planted a garden eastward, in Eden (Gen.2:8). The Hebrew word for garden is Gan and of this word Gesenius says, "A garden, especially one planted with trees (properly a place protected with a fence)." Thus when God planted a garden in Eden He made a within and a without. The garden was an enclosure and beyond it lay the field, the world. Into the garden He put the man (Adam) that He had made of the dust of the ground outside the garden, and his work was to dress and keep the garden. In the garden was a test of his loyalty to the LORD God and obedience to His word in regard to the tree of the knowledge of good and evil. He disobeyed, sinned and was driven out of the garden to the outside (Genesis, chapters 2 and 3).

Similarly, we have a within and without in connection with the church of God in Corinth. See chapter 5 as to God's judgement on the brother guilty of fornication, and in 1 Cor.5:12,13 we read, "For what have I to do with judging them that are without? Do not ye judge them that are within, whereas them that are without God judgeth? Put away the wicked man from among yourselves." Some misinformed people think that those within are saints in the Body of Christ, and those without are unsaved people. Does sin invade the Body of Christ? If it does then the Gates of Hades have prevailed, and the Lord will never be able to present the Church to Himself without spot or wrinkle or any such thing (Matt.16:18; Eph.5:27). The church of God in Corinth was a place of judgement, for sin might and did find a place therein and had to be dealt with, and the sinning brother put outside. But he was not put outside the Church which is Christ's Body. Within and without referred to here have nothing to do with saved people who are all members of the Body of Christ; it is truth proper to the church and churches of God.

1 Cor.3:7,8,9

Paul says that the workmen whom God uses are not anything, whether they are those who plant or those who water; God is all, who makes things to grow, even as He did the work in Corinth. The planter and the waterer were one, that is, as yoked together in the same work. This thought of oneness is seen in the work of the Remnant which returned from Babylon to rebuild the house of God in Jerusalem. In Ezra 3:1 we are told that "the people gathered themselves together as one man to Jerusalem." Then in verse 9 we read, "Then stood Jeshua with his sons and his brethren, Kadmiel and his sons, the sons of Judah, together (as one), to have the oversight of the workmen in the house of God."

Thus the people were one and the overseers were one. It is only thus that God's work can go on in prosperity. Then as to the recommencement of divine service after the house of God has been completed, we read, "For the priests and the Levites had purified themselves together (as one); all of them were pure: and they killed the Passover for all the children of the captivity, and for their brethren the priests, and for themselves" (Ezra 6:20). Although the workers are one in being yoked together, each one shall receive his own reward and the reward will be determined according to the amount of labour done. This is only just. Many today want equal pay whether they are idlers or workers. This is not how God will reward His saints. Little labour will mean little reward. Verse 9 should not be read as in the AV/KJV, "We are labourers together with God." The RV is correct, "We are God's fellow-workers."

Paul and Apollos did not labour together with God, but they were fellow-workers owned by God and used by Him. The workers were God's as was also the husbandry, the tilled land where the plants were planted together to bear fruit, and they were also the building, the temple of God (verses 16,17), in which God dwelt. The husbandry and the building describe the church of God in Corinth, but the words convey two different ideas, that of a garden and of a house.

1 Cor.3:10-11

Paul describes himself as a wise master-builder (Gk. architekton) who laid a foundation. The building of verse 9 required, as all buildings do, a foundation. He laid the foundation of the doctrine relative to the Person of Jesus Christ, on the basis of which the saints in Corinth were gathered together as the church of God in that city, a called-out and gathered-together people. The teaching of Jesus Christ and the Person of Jesus Christ are one and indivisible. We know nothing of Jesus Christ apart from the teaching or doctrine of Christ (2 Jn 9,10) as contained in the Scriptures. There are no extant authoritative records relative to His Person and teaching other than those which are contained in the Holy Scriptures.

Paul laid in Corinth the same foundation as God laid in the heavenly Zion (Heb.12:22; 1 Pet.2:4-6; Isa.28:16; Ps.2:6,7), when He raised and set His Son at His right hand. He was the Stone whom the builders rejected who has been made the Head of the corner (Ps.118:22,23). Peter identified the builders as the Jewish leaders, Annas, Caiaphas, John and Alexander and the kindred of the high priest, with the rulers and elders (Acts 4:5-12). In Acts 4:11,12, Peter associates salvation with the Stone which the Jewish leaders rejected, and says, "In none other is there salvation." But in 1 Pet.2:1-10 he is writing of a redeemed and born-again people, who have tasted that the Lord is gracious, coming to Him, not for salvation, but to be built up a spiritual house, to be a holy priesthood, to offer up spiritual sacrifices acceptable to God through Jesus Christ. This offering of spiritual sacrifices by those who are in this spiritual house is possible because God has laid this precious elect Stone in Zion.

Jesus Christ is the Stone of sure foundation. He has all authority in heaven and on earth. The heavenly hosts are ruled by Him, and it is God's will that saved people on earth should be together in subjection to Him to obey His word and will. Such was Paul's work in Corinth and in other Gentile cities. He laid the one and only possible foundation. Another foundation can no man lay, even as there is no other gospel than that which Paul preached (Gal.1:6-8). There is one Saviour for the sinner and one Lord for the saint.

1 Cor.3:12,13

Here Paul warns all teachers who come after him about the character of their teaching, that it must be in accordance with the character and quality of the foundation which he laid. Six materials are indicated by Paul, three of which fire cannot consume, and three which are highly combustible. Much wood, hay, and stubble, which are the product of nature, may be heaped up at a small price. Gold and silver are precious metals, and these with precious stones occupy little space. A little well done by the Spirit's power will be found to be better than much that is the result of fleshly and natural activity. The fiery trial of the day of Christ shall declare what has been of God and what has not. We must not conclude that the gold, etc., are saints, and the wood, etc., are sinners. There will be no sinners at the judgement-seat of Christ, which judgement-seat is envisaged here, and saints will not be tested in fire at that judgement-seat, though their works will. Further, the works of believers who are not in a church of God, and who have not been building on the foundation such as Paul laid, are not contemplated here, though they will undoubtedly be at the judgement-seat of Christ. To be in the building which is built on the foundation which Paul laid (verses 9-11), is of very great importance.

1 Cor.3:14,15

This trial is not one of punishments, but of rewards or loss of rewards. Salvation, eternal life, righteousness through faith, are gifts, not rewards. Here, at the judgement-seat of Christ (Rom.14:10,11,12; 1 Cor.4:3-5; 2 Cor.5:10), the Lord will be dealing with His servants. The Lord said, "He that doeth the truth cometh to the light, that his works may be made manifest, that they have been wrought in God" (Jn 3:21). "God is a consuming fire" (Heb.12:29). What has been wrought in God, God will not consume. If the builder's work is burned, the builder himself shall be saved, but so as through fire. The builder will neither be saved nor lost by his own work, but is saved by the work of Christ. He will stand in the righteousness of Christ, though his own righteousness may be consumed, and nothing may be left which will adorn the Bride on her marriage day, for she is adorned with fine linen which is the righteous acts of the saints (Rev.19:8). What a loss that will be!

1 Cor.3:16,17

The church of God in Corinth was "temple of God." The RV says "a temple," and the AV/KJV "the temple," but there is no definite article before temple in the Greek. When the definite article is omitted it is the character of the thing that is in view. The church of God in Corinth was temple of God, and each church was, similarly, temple of God. All the churches of God together formed the temple of God. Verse 17, referring to what has been described in the previous verse as "temple of God," speaks of "the temple of God." A Greek scholar says, "The article is inserted in the renewed mention of a person or thing." Thus the use of the article here is not in the sense that the church in Corinth was "the" temple, as though there was no other. It is necessary to distinguish between what is said in the above verses about the church in Corinth being temple of God and the body of the believer being temple of the Holy Spirit (1 Cor.6:19).

"Know ye not that your body is a temple of the Holy Spirit which is in you?" This is true of the bodies of all believers in this dispensation, and the believer is to glorify God in his body. Paul in 3:17 says, "If any man destroyeth the temple of God, him shall God destroy." The temple of God can be destroyed (or currupted) by introducing wrong doctrine or practice. The same word used here (Gk. phtheiro, to spoil, corrupt, destroy) is used of good manners, in 1 Cor.15:33, "Evil company doth corrupt good manners." If good manners are corrupted, where are they? They do not exist! Even so, if a church of God is corrupted, it will cease to exist as temple of God. If any man sets out on a course of corrupting God's temple, then, it is said that God will corrupt him. God's temple was the church in Corinth which was a habitation of God in the Spirit (Eph.2:22).

1 Cor.3:18,19,20

Here Paul administers a warning about pride which had manifested itself in the church in Corinth in their preferring one above another. A believer must humble himself to be exalted, empty himself of self to be filled, become a fool to become wise. Such as account themselves to be wise as to this age, are fools with God. "For the wisdom of the world is foolishness with God." Psalm 49 is a psalm to all the inhabitants of the world. In it the ways of men are clearly defined, ways which are the same today as they were thousands of years ago, men, their wealth, their houses, their lands, the praise of the rich and well-to-do, all pass in review under the pen of inspiration. But what is the end? It is this, "Man that is in honour, and understandeth not, is like the beasts that perish" (verse 20). Though their way is one of folly, "yet after them men approve their sayings" (verse 13). Who are the wise and what is wisdom?

"The fear of the Lord, that is wisdom; and to depart from evil is understanding" (Job 28:28).

1 Cor.3:21,22,23

Why should man glory in man when he is but a potsherd among the potsherds of the earth? (Isa.45:9). Let man's boast be in the Lord (1 Cor.1:31) who is from everlasting to everlasting and who will not give His glory to another, and rightly so (Isa.42:8). What an endowment God gave to His saints in such teachers as Paul, Apollos and Cephas, for their enrichment in spiritual and eternal things! Such were some of His gifts to men (Eph.4:8-13). As with the apostles and other servants of God, whose work was the reaching with the gospel those who were God's by divine election and the perfecting those who were His by Spirit-given ministry, so all things subserve their purpose in the divine economy for the well-being of God's saints. Each plays its part, the world, life and death, things present and coming things, all are so arranged by God for the good of His own.

It is a sublime conception and raises God's saints to an eminence which should humble them before God, that all this has been arranged by God for their sake. But in contrast to what is the portion of God's saints, Christ is not said to be theirs, but rather that they are His. They are His purchased possession, and Christ is God's: Christ, the divine-human Mediator, co-equal and co-eternal with God, yet a partaker of blood and flesh like unto the children. In the light of all this review, how foolish of men to prefer one servant above another, seeing that each is possessed by all!

COMMENTARY ON 1 CORINTHIANS 4

1 Cor.4:1,2

Paul says, "Let a man," or more correctly "Let man," in contradistinction to God who had made these servants of His what they were, "so account of us, as of ministers (Gk. huperetes, under-rower, under-seaman, underling or attendant) of Christ, and stewards (an overseer of a man's affairs, an agent or steward, one to whom things are entrusted for the benefit of others) of the mysteries of God." Mystery (Gk. musterion) here means, "Some sacred thing hidden or secret, which is naturally unknown to human reason, and is only known by the revelation of God"; the word is derived from mueo, to imitate, from muo, to shut (the mouth). Many of God's secrets were revealed to the apostles.

Thus we read of "the Mystery of God, even Christ" (Col.2:2); "the Mystery of godliness," which is Christ manifested in the flesh (1 Tim.3:16); "the mystery of the gospel" (Eph.6:19); "the mystery of Christ," which is the Church which is His Body (Eph.3:4); "the mystery of His (God's) will" (Eph.1:9); "the mysteries of the kingdom of heaven" (Matt.13:11); "the mysteries of the kingdom of God" (Lk.8:10); "the mystery of the faith" (1 Tim.3:9); the mystery of the hardening in part of Israel (Rom.11:25); "Mystery, Babylon the great" (Rev.17:5); "the mystery of iniquity" or lawlessness (2 Thess.2:7); only the Lord, Paul and John use the word musterion; the Lord three, Paul twenty and John four times. Faithfulness is an outstanding character required in a steward; one who can be trusted in the discharge of his duties. See the parable of the unjust steward in Lk.16:1-13.

1 Cor.4:3,4

God's stewards should be judged by their Divine Master as to their work and not by men. This does not touch upon the subject of the matter of spiritual or moral delinquency. Paul accounted it a small matter to be judged by men as to his work or apostleship. In that he knew nothing against himself. This again does not touch upon the trouble he had with sin in the flesh, as in Rom.7:7-25, from which the holiest of God's servants are not exempt, which, in 2 Chron.6:29, Solomon called "his own plague." Paul was being judged by the Cor.in what he called, "man's day" (4:3, AV/KJV), that is, the present day. After this will come "the day of Christ," the day when Christ shall judge and reward His saints, as Paul refers to here. After that will come "the day of the Lord," when the Lord shall judge the world. Though Paul was not conscious of any failure in the discharge of his work, yet he was not his own judge, and was not justified in consequence. His judge was the Lord, whose knowledge was far in excess of the acuteness of the human conscience, however active.

1 Cor.4:5

"Judge nothing" must not be lifted out of its context or it would lead to cancelling out other portions of the word, such as, 1 Cor.5:12, "Do not ye judge them that are within?" and also verse 3, "I verily ... have already ... judged him that hath so wrought this thing." The saints were also to judge wrongs between brethren, see 1 Cor.6:1-8: The Lord is the judge of the work of His servants, and that He will do at His judgement-seat (Bema, a step, an elevated place ascended by steps, a tribunal, not a throne) (2 Cor.5:10). Here the saints of this dispensation of grace will appear, and there will be brought to light the hidden things of darkness, and also the counsels of the heart which gave rise to the acts done. Solemn day for all! Each man who is worthy of praise will receive his due meed of praise from God.

1 Cor.4:6,7

As we have already indicated, in our note on 1 Cor.1:12, Paul was using his name and that of Apollos to show the evil that existed among the Cor.in their being puffed up for the one against the other, which is the seedbed of schism. Both he who admits the thought of carnal admiration for others, and he who enjoys being admired, are wrong. This course feeds pride and self-conceit in the human heart. Paul uses the Greek word phusioo, rendered "Puffed up," which means to breathe, to inflate, which means to inflate with pride and vanity. To follow this course is to go beyond what is written in the Scriptures. This has been one of the fatal sources of divisions amongst Christians. Paul writes, in 2 Cor.8:18, "We have sent together with him the brother whose praise in the gospel is spread through all the churches," but what he writes of in the verses above is simply natural pride and vanity in the human heart undisciplined by grace, for what has any one but what he has received through God's grace? If God has bestowed a greater gift upon one than another, it is no cause for glorying, as though the gift proceeded from oneself. It needs a humble heart to bear the weight of a great gift.

1 Cor.4:8

Here Paul alludes to what he wrote in 1:5, that in everything they were enriched in Christ Jesus, in all utterance and all knowledge. They had made great progress in divine things since their conversion and the planting of the church of God in Corinth, but, alas, their pride and carnality had also increased. They were reigning as spiritual kings. Paul wished that the reigning time had arrived, that he might reign with them, but it was suffering time, not the reigning time. The following verse shows this clearly. Their reigning was false and groundless.

1 Cor.4:9,10

Here Paul portrays a procession of doomed men, and last of all God has set forth the apostles. They were a spectacle (Gk. theatron, a theatre, a place where the public games were held, here it is a public spectacle, as if exhibited in a theatre) to an audience of the world, angels and men. It is a true saying that "the world persecutes living saints and praises dead ones." All Christendom today wishes to be thought of as being apostolic, but if the apostles walked into the religious world today with the message that they spoke when they were here, they would be given like treatment as they received in the past, and so also would Christ Himself. The Corinthians were wise in Christ, strong, and glorious, but the apostles were fools for Christ's sake, weak and dishonoured. What irony is in the words of Paul!

1 Cor.4:11,12,13

Paul was writing, as a spiritual father, to the Corinthians, not to make them ashamed of their behaviour, but to admonish (Gk. noutheteo, "to place upon the mind" something that would prove a corrective, hence the word means, to reprove, to instruct, to warn) them, for they were his beloved children, begotten through the gospel. As we think of the suffering of these servants of Christ we cannot forbear from saying, "Blessed men!" James says, "We call them blessed that endured." Here were men who went their way to heaven in privation and destitution, for even as he wrote, Paul says, they suffered hunger, thirst, nakedness, were buffeted, and had no certain dwelling place, no home of their own. To maintain themselves they wrought with their own hands while they preached, as he wrote to both the Corinthians and the Thessalonians (2 Cor.11:7; Acts 18:3; 2 Thess.3:8). "Being persecuted, we endure; being defamed, we intreat." It was in their case a kiss for a blow, a smile for a frown, love for hatred, and though poor they were making many rich. Such was the way that the apostles went as they followed after their Divine Master. Paul spoke of the apostles as the filth (Gk. perikatharma, the sweepings, refuse, filth), and the offscouring (Gk. peripsema, the scrapings, scum) of all things. What a description! That the world should view the greatest men of this dispensation in this way is an addition to its disgrace in regard to the way it treated the Lord of all Himself!

1 Cor.4:14,15,16

Though Paul's letters were weighty and powerful, yet he was one of the most loving and kindliest of men, one in whose heart the love of God was shed abroad. His object in writing as he did was to admonish, not to make them ashamed. They might have ten thousand tutors in Christ, yet they had not many fathers. (Tutor, Gk. paidagogos, "among the Greeks properly signified a servant, whose business it was constantly to attend on his young master, to watch over his behaviour, and particularly to lead him to and from school and the place of exercise. These were generally slaves, imperious and severe.") Paul claims to have begotten the Corinthians through the gospel. All may not have been born again through his ministry, as he joins Apollos with himself in this work (3:5). He calls on his spiritual children to be imitators of himself.

1 Cor.4:17

Paul sent Timothy to Corinth to remind the saints of his godly living, which he calls his ways which be in Christ. Timothy was like the Corinthians, in that he too had been begotten again under the apostle's ministry; he calls him his beloved and faithful child. But notice he uses the description "in the Lord," showing that Timothy was faithful in his subjection to the Lord. It is possible to be a child of God "in Christ," yet not "in the Lord," that is, not subject to the Lord's will. Paul's ways were according to the doctrine he taught. Moreover, the doctrine he taught was the same in every church. He did not suit his teaching to the tastes and fancies of the saints in the different churches. This is most important in those who would teach others. God's teaching was the Lord's teaching (Jn 7:16,17). The Lord's teaching was the teaching of the apostles (Matt.28:19,20; Acts 2:42). Similarly it is said of the Lord, that He began to do and to teach until the day in which He was received up (Acts 1:1,2).

1 Cor.4:18,19,20,21

In his sending Timothy to Corinth, it was not that Paul feared to go himself. Some were puffed up with pride, and, perchance, thought that Paul would not come to Corinth. But Paul intended to go there, if it was the Lord's will. If and when he did, he would not know the word of them that were puffed up, but his word would be in power, "for," said he, "the kingdom of God is not in word, but in power." In the kingdom of God there must be power to put wrong things right, or the rule of God does not exist at all; this must be true of any kingdom that is worthy of the name of a kingdom. A kingdom that exists in word only, where there is no power to put the law into effect, is anarchy and not a kingdom. Paul puts it to them to decide in what spirit he is to come, whether with the rod of discipline or in love and in a spirit of meekness. Their behaviour and attitude to the principles of righteousness would determine this.

COMMENTARY ON 1 CORINTHIANS 5

1 Cor.5:1,2

The report had reached Paul that fornication was actually among (En, in, among them collectively) them. It was a case of serious incest, of the sort as was not among (En) the Gentiles, that one in the church had his father's wife, presumably his step-mother. Though this sin of serious irregularity existed, the Corinthians were so carnal and puffed up, that they did not mourn that he that was so wicked should be removed from their midst. This is yet another instance in which Paul charges upon the Corinthian believers that they were puffed up with pride.

1 Cor.5:3,4,5

This sin under the law was punishable by death (Lev.20:11), and such as committed it were cursed by the law (Deut.27:20). The utmost penalty that can be inflicted in this dispensation of grace on a believer in a church of God is excommunication. This judgement should have been imposed upon this man by the elders of the church in Corinth by their calling upon the church to put him away, but they had failed in their duty, hence the need for Paul to call upon them to carry out the proper judgement in this case. Paul's judgement is given, though he was absent in body, he was present in spirit.

"Present in spirit" does not mean, present in thought or in memory, but that he was present with the actual knowledge of facts as they existed, and hence with an actual knowledge of the facts he was able to give a correct and just judgement. All judgement is based on facts. Paul's judgement was the judgement of God. "Ye being gathered together, and my spirit, with the power of our Lord Jesus" is a parenthetical clause. Paul's judgement was – "In the name of our Lord Jesus ... to deliver such a one unto Satan." This delivering of the man unto Satan was to be done when the church was gathered together, and they were empowered in their action by the spirit of the apostle and the power of the Lord Jesus.

In 1 Tim.1:20 Paul tells of his having delivered Hymenaeus and Alexander unto Satan, but in their case it was that they might be taught not to blaspheme. In Corinth the sinning brother was delivered unto Satan for the destruction of the flesh, that the spirit might be saved in the day of the Lord Jesus. The day of the Lord Jesus is the present day, not the day of Christ when the Lord shall come for His saints of the Church. We know that the day of the Lord's coming will see the end of the flesh with all its sinful emotions for God's children. Then we shall be delivered from the body of this death (Rom.7:24,25). But the destruction of the flesh is effected, in 1 Cor.5, by the man being delivered unto Satan. That destruction is present, not future, and so is the saving of the man's spirit to be a present experience. The destruction of the flesh and the saving of the spirit synchronize. The repentance and restoration of this man is dealt with in 2 Cor.2:1-11, at which time his spirit was saved.

1 Cor.5:6,7,8

Instead of being humbled that such a sin existed among them, they were glorying in their shame. This leaven of immoral conduct leavened the assembly. It was as the sin of Achan the troubler, in connection with which the LORD said, "Israel hath sinned," not Achan hath sinned. Israel was responsible to deal with the sin of Achan, which they did. Even so it was the responsibility of the church in Corinth to purge out the old leaven of immoral conduct by putting the man away. Paul speaks here of the leaven of immoral conduct, and in Gal.5:9 he speaks of the leaven of false doctrine, particularly the false teaching relative to circumcision and law-keeping as being necessary to salvation. The principle is the same in both cases, "A little leaven leaveneth the whole lump."

Its power to corrupt when put in cereal products is irresistible. The church of God in Corinth when it was planted is compared by Paul to a new lump of unleavened dough. A parallel may be seen in the fact that the people of Israel, when they were redeemed from Egypt, carried out their unleavened dough in their kneading troughs (Ex.12:34).

As Israel were redeemed through the Passover, even so we have been delivered through our Passover, even Christ. Therefore we are to keep the feast (Gk. heortazomen, we should "keep festival," RV marg., which gives the correct meaning here), not eating literally, therefore does not refer to the loaf of the Lord's Remembrance. This festival is one of unleavened bread, not with the leaven of immoral conduct, the old leaven, nor with the leaven of malice and wickedness, but with unleavened bread of sincerity and truth. This is the unleavened bread of today with which festival is to be kept.

1 Cor.5:9,10,11

Paul does not say, "I am writing to you," but "I wrote (Aorist tense) unto you." There is nothing in this epistle before chapter 5 or after on the subject of company-keeping with fornicators. It is therefore clear that he had written an epistle to the Corinthians before this one. His reference to fornicators was not to the fornicators of this world. Fornicators, covetous, extortioners, idolators, were then so numerous in Corinth, and still are in this world, that to be free from them they would need to go out of the world. Paul, who wrote before unto them, says, "Now I write unto you not to keep company, if any man that is named a brother be a fornicator, etc."

Saints are not at liberty to treat a brother in the way Paul describes until the church, led by its overseers, deals with a brother for any one of these sins and puts him away from the church. Then the saints are under the obligation of treating him as Paul commands, and his command is the commandment of the Lord. There is to be no company-keeping by any saints with a man judged guilty of one of these sins. Such a course would thwart the course of justice and hinder repentance on the man's part, and also hinder his restoration to the Lord and His people. See how the Corinthians showed themselves to be clear in this matter, in 2 Cor.7:5-16: The Greek word for "to keep company" is sunanamignumi, which means, to associate with, to have familiar intercourse. Eating here means eating in general, and does not simply mean of the loaf on Lord's day in remembrance of the Lord. Eating with is one of the strongest evidences of fellowship. Where family relationships exist, eating may not have the meaning of association or company- keeping as is here indicated.

1 Cor.5:12,13

Here we have "within" and "without." Within and without what? Quite evidently it is within the church of God in Corinth and without that gathering of saints, the people who are addressed in 1 Cor.1:2: Saints cannot put a saint outside of the Church which is Christ's Body. They had no part in putting them into the Body and they can have no part in putting anyone outside of it. But saints have a part in adding one to the number of those together in a church of God, and consequently where sin of such a nature as is spoken of in the previous verses exists, they are responsible to put the person away. Saints in a church of God are responsible to judge wrong-doing in their midst, as Paul asks, "Do not ye judge them that are within?" Scattered saints cannot possibly carry out what is here enjoined upon those who are gathered together. See note on 1 Cor. 3:4,5,6.

COMMENTARY ON 1 CORINTHIANS 6

1 Cor.6:1,2

Paul dares any one to have such self-confidence in any matter against his neighbour in the church in Corinth as to go to law before the unrighteous, in the courts of judicature among the Gentiles. The course in such matters is to have them settled by arbitration by saints and not by unjustified men. He tells them that the saints shall judge the world (Dan.7:18,22,27), and if the saints in Corinth, with others like themselves, were to have this great responsibility, were they unworthy and incapable in judgements of smallest things? The things between saints are deemed to be among the smallest matters, yet their settlement is necessary to peace in the church.

1 Cor.6:3,4

Are these angels in view in this verse good or bad angels? There are the angels that sinned (2 Pet.2:4), and there are the angels that have not sinned. Hence, it appears, angels which have not sinned will have no need to be judged. Thus we conclude that the angels who will be judged will be those that sinned. Paul writes, in Rom.16:20, of the God of peace bruising Satan under their feet shortly. If saints have to do with Satan in this way in the future, when the final victory over Satan, as is indicated in this verse, will be realized, it is no great stretch of imagination that in some sense, not here revealed, the saints will judge the fallen angels who aligned themselves with Satan in his rebellion against God. This rebellion they will carry on until the end, when the suffering of eternal fire will be theirs. Seeing that saints shall judge angels in the future, how much more the things of this life? Then the question is put by Paul, that if we have tribunals in this life, who are the persons to give judgement at such tribunals? Are those to judge who are of no account or the least esteemed in the church? Such a question has only to be asked to be answered. Those who should be set to give judgement between their brethren ought to be the best men available.

1 Cor.6:5,6,7,8

Paul sought to shame the Corinthians by his suggestive question on the point of their setting up the least esteemed in the church to judge, whereas he asks whether they were unable to find one wise man among themselves who could judge between his brethren. But brother going to law with brother before unbelievers was a defect in them and a blemish on the church's testimony. If they were unable to find one wise man among them to decide between his brethren, then his mind was put in the form of a question, Why not suffer wrong? why not be defrauded? Then he accused them of doing wrong and defrauding, that is, those who were dragging their brethren before the judgement seats of the unrighteous.

1 Cor.6:9,10

Paul here amplifies the list of sins mentioned in 5:11, for all of which excommunication is the punishment. The kingdom of God is a present inheritance, and a condition of inheritance is regeneration (Jn 3:3,5), plus righteousness, that is the doing of what is right, practical righteousness, in contrast to imputed righteousness (Matt.6:33; Rom.14:17). "He that doeth righteousness is righteous, even as He is righteous: he that doeth sin is of the devil" (1 Jn 3:7,8). "Through many tribulations we must enter into the kingdom of God" (Acts 14:22), shows that we do not enter the kingdom of God once for all, as is the case of such as are translated into the kingdom of the Son of His love (Col.1:13). Paul in Eph.5:5, uses somewhat similar words to those contained in the verses which we are considering: "For this ye know of a surety, that no fornicator, nor unclean person, nor covetous man, which is an idolater, hath any inheritance in the kingdom of Christ and God."

Fornicators, adulterers, effeminate, and abusers of themselves with men, are such as practise various types of sexual sins, all of which are contrary to the word of God, sins which God will judge in this life with most serious punishment. Idolaters, thieves, covetous and extortioners, are such as practise different forms of covetousness, a lust which is deeply ingrained in the greed of man's lustful nature. Drunkards are a selfish class of persons whose god is the belly, and children have suffered grievously from this lust in a father or mother. Rev.ilers or railers are persons with a distorted mind and a perverted tongue. Can such sins be committed by persons who are born again? The answer is, alas, yes. Persons characterized by such sins cannot continue to retain their place in a church of God, which is the local expression of the kingdom of God.

1 Cor.6:11

Such sins enumerated in the previous verses were characteristic of some of the Corinthians, but, says Paul, "Ye washed yourselves" (RV marg.). The verb "washed" is in the middle voice, which shows that it was something which they did for themselves, and that by the application of the water of the word to their habits, the washing was outward and manward. It was like what Ananias said to Paul after his conversion, "And now why tarriest thou? arise, and be baptized, and wash away your sins, calling on His name" (Acts 22:16). Paul's sins had been cleansed away by the blood of Christ three days before as he lay on the Damascus road. But he washed away his sins before men by his obedience to the truth of God in baptism. By this men could see that he was no longer a persecuting Pharisee, but a disciple of the Lord Jesus; this they saw when in his baptism he called upon the name of the Lord whom he had previously despised and hated.

Peter also says, "Seeing ye have purified your souls in your obedience to the truth unto unfeigned love of the brethren, love one another from the heart fervently" (1 Pet.1:22). Thus it was the Corinthians washed themselves by their obedience to the truth, in that they ceased their former evil practices and became Christ-like in their behaviour. They were also sanctified (set apart) in Christ Jesus, Christ became their sanctification (1:2,30). They were also justified (declared righteous), Christ was their righteousness (1:30). These acts were done for them once for all, in the name of the Lord Jesus, and in (by the action and energy of) the Spirit of God.

1 Cor.6:12,13

It is not lawful to do what is unlawful. What Paul is dealing with is Christian liberty from all legal bondage and the restrictions imposed by men in their religious systems. Such impose systems of "severity to the body ... not of any value against the indulgence of the flesh" (Col.2:23). They were often simply evidences of will-worship. Such were the systems of the Pharisees, the Essenes, and the Stoics. Paul wrote to the Galatians and said, "Ye, brethren, were called for freedom; only use not your freedom for an occasion to the flesh" (Gal.5:13). Though Paul could act with freedom, yet his actions might not be expedient to the profit of others. This he deals with in chapters 8 and 10: Though all things were lawful, yet he would so conduct himself in the use of things so as not to be brought under the power of any, but would remain a free man. He would not indulge his appetite so as to become a gross feeder, nor use spirituous beverages so as to be brought under the power of alcohol.

He would in regard to bodily appetites buffet his body and bring it into bondage, and not allow the body to bring him into bondage to its appetites and lusts (1 Cor.9:27). He would be under the authority of things. How swiftly the flesh is ready to take advantage through the demands of the body to filch from the Christian his liberty! Disciples are not to be like the Gentiles whose main quest is what they shall eat and what they shall drink and wherewith they shall be clothed (Lk.12:29). The time will come when, as Paul says, God will bring both the belly and meats to nought. Eating and drinking, digestion and assimilation are but temporary expedients, for we look for a glorious bodily change which will be in agreement with a perfect state. Then Paul tells us of the proper use of the body, that it is not for fornication, but for the Lord. Even the lawful married state is but temporary. The body is necessary in the divine economy of things for the functioning of man on earth, but its high purpose is for the Lord, that in the human body of saints He may be glorified.

1 Cor.6:14

This verse confirms what Paul says as to the body of the saints, that the body is for the Lord, that through it both now, and for ever in its renewed state, God's will might be done. "The Lord for the body"; in all its needs He is the true and full answer, whether in life or in death or in that life that lies beyond resurrection. God, who raised our Lord Jesus from the dead, will raise us up also, and in bodies raised and changed like unto His we shall rise to meet Him in the air. Such considerations should elevate our thoughts as to these bodies in which we dwell, as to the proper use to which they are to be put.

1 Cor.6:15

The whole being of a believer is a member of Christ, but here Paul centres our thoughts on that part of us – the body, not upon the soul or spirit – as though they were excluded from membership with Christ. "The Christ," as in 1 Cor.12:12, signifies Christ and His members. The members of Christ are joined to Him who is the Head in an indivisible and abiding unity which will last for ever. Paul asks, Shall I take away the members of Christ, and make them members of a harlot? This means the members of Christ as viewed from the point of view of their bodies. The union of two persons in the consummation of marriage, according to God's ordinance, abides during the lifetime of the parties, but, alas, it is often affected by lewd and irregular intercourse. God forbids this, and says that He will judge such sinners. Believers should ever remember the bond of life and love which exists between Christ and them, and use their bodies for lawful and holy purposes and not in irregularities condemned by God.

1 Cor.6:16,17

The word "joined" in this verse is from the Greek word kollao, which means "to be glued together," and is the same word, though in a different form, rendered "cleave" in Matt.19:5; Mk.10:7, showing what is to be the effect in the consummation of marriage. The Hebrew word for "cleave" in Gen.2:24, is of similar meaning. In Eph.5:31,32, it is used to show the cleaving together of Christ and His members. True marriage implies more than a mere physical union. Woman was made for man, and was the answer to man's complex needs, spiritually, mentally and physically; she was his complement to complete him. The mere joining of a man to a harlot in illicit intercourse is but a physical, despicable and criminal act of the flesh, a consummation of what is proper to marriage where no marriage exists, and has no answer in the realm of what is mental and spiritual. The twain become one flesh for a moment's carnal pleasure.

In contrast to this, he that is joined (glued) to the Lord is one spirit. Here is the higher and fuller meaning of what God had in view in Gen.2:24, an abiding spiritual union. This union in spirit between the Lord and His members will abide when what pertains to the flesh now will have faded into oblivion, for the joys of spiritual union shall never end. Though the Church is already joined in its members to Christ the Head, the complete Church, the Bride of the Lamb, will not be married to the Lamb until the time of Rev.19:7,8, which time is between the coming of the Lord to the air for the Church and His coming to earth as the Son of Man to reign. At the time the Church is married to Christ, a matter of public joy in heaven, in contrast to the uniting in secret of each member one by one to the Head now, the people of Israel will be undergoing the fearsome persecution of antichrist on earth. Israel forms no part of the Church, the Bride of the Lamb.

1 Cor.6:18

No man dare stay to fight fornication. Safety is in flight and not in fight, as Joseph fled from Potiphar's lustful wife. Where Judah fell (Gen.38), Joseph rose supreme (Gen.39). What does Paul mean when he says, "Every sin that a man doeth is without the body"? "Without" is from the Greek word ektos, which means on the outside of or exterior to. If, as some have said, "the body" here means the same as "his own body" in this verse, how are we to understand that the sins of drunkenness, addiction to drugs, gluttony, smoking (especially such as inhale tobacco smoke into their lungs exposing themselves to lung cancer) are without the human body? Surely the introduction of alcohol in quantity, the poisons of opium, etc., nicotine, and toxins arising from overeating, are all sins against one's own body, by introducing things within the body that should not be there. These, as well as fornication, constitute sinning against one's body.

"Without the body," means, in my opinion, that sins of all kinds whether they be against one's body or otherwise, are outside of the Body of Christ. Even though we may sin against our own bodies, this sin is not introduced into the Body of Christ. The reason for this is that Christ is the Saviour or Preserver of the Body (Eph.5:23). His preserving care for the Body is as mysterious as the preserving of the redeemed soul of each saved person from the effects of sins of thought, word and deed; a profound mystery indeed! Though it is true, of all saved persons, that in me, that is in my flesh, there dwelleth no good thing, yet the redeemed soul is free for ever from the defiling effects of sin. Such things, as Peter said of the writings of Paul, may be hard to be understood (2 Pet.3:15,16), yet they are not untrue.

1 Cor.6:19,20

Here is yet another fact relative to the body of believers. We have seen that (1) the body is for the Lord and the Lord for the body, (2) that the bodies of believers are members of Christ, and (3) now we are told that "your body is a temple of the Holy Spirit." The body which was once put to an evil use is now a temple of the Holy Spirit. What wondrous grace for this Divine Person to indwell the bodies of saints! God does not speak of temples; the plural, "temples," is never used of either the bodies of saints or of the churches of God (1 Cor.3:16,17; 2 Cor.6:16; Eph.2:21,22). Each believer's body is a temple of the Holy Spirit from the moment of regeneration, but this must not be confused with the church of God being called a temple of God. The church of God as a temple of God demands the regeneration of each individual therein, also that such must be baptized in water and added together (Acts 2:41,42).

All the churches of God must be in one Fellowship, that of God's Son Jesus Christ our Lord (1 Cor.1:9). The believer is not his own property; he is a purchased slave, and therefore he is to glorify God in His Body. He is sealed with the Holy Spirit unto the day of redemption, when his body will be redeemed at the Lord's coming (Eph.1:13,14; 4:30; Rom.8:23). The believer in his mortal body should find an example in glorifying God from that of the Lord, who said, "I glorified Thee on the earth, having accomplished the work which Thou has given Me to do" (Jn 17:4).

COMMENTARY ON 1 CORINTHIANS 7

1 Cor.7:1,2

The Corinthians had evidently written to Paul on the subject of marriage. Paul with his high conception of the purpose of God in redeemed people, that God's purpose in them is not generation and the procreation of the race, but regeneration which is effected by the spread of the gospel, led him to conclude that it was good for a man not to touch a woman. When the Lord had answered the Pharisees on the question of divorce, and showed to them the abiding character of marriage, according to God's institution, the disciples said, "If the case of the man is so with his wife, it is not expedient to marry." He answered them, "All men cannot receive this saying, but they to whom it is given."

Then He spoke of different kinds of eunuchs, and lastly He spoke of such as make themselves eunuchs for the kingdom of heaven's sake (Matt.19:10-12), men who remain unmarried for the spreading of the gospel without hindrance. Such, I judge, was Paul. Side by side with what Paul says about a man not touching a woman, he speaks of the grave dangers of a celibate life, he said that each should have his own wife and the woman her own husband.

1 Cor.7:3,4,5

Cohabitation is the due of husband and wife to each other, each having authority over the body of the other. Hence there is to be no defrauding of each other's rights, except for a season, that they may have leisure for prayer. This course of being free from the lower bodily desires was that the higher spiritual exercises connected with prayer should not be hindered. Thereafter they could come together again. All is to be done in a godly manner by consent, so that Satan might not gain any access through the incontinency of the flesh to tempt them to irregularities.

1 Cor.7:6,7

Paul gives wise advice, but not by God's commandment. He reverts to what he said in verse 1, saying that he would have all men as himself. All men must be limited to saved men. He would have saved men to be free from the burdens and responsibilities that marriage incurs, though, of course, marriage has its compensations, if one's partner is a true helpmeet in spiritual things. Paul recognized that each man had his gift from God, one to remain single and the other to marry. His words give no sanction for societies of celibate priests, monks and nuns. Such institutions of men have no sanction from the Scriptures whatever.

1 Cor.7:8,9

Paul gives advice to the unmarried of both sexes, and singles out widows particularly, that it should be good for them to remain unmarried like himself. But where there is incontinency or lack of self-control, it is better to marry than to be inflamed with lust.

1 Cor.7:10,11

Paul turns to married people, and here he speaks with the Lord's authority, and he says that they are not to leave each other. This is the truth of all Scripture. But if a wife departs from her husband, because of certain serious events or conditions, she is to remain unmarried, or else be reconciled to her husband. Remarriage for Christian people is not allowed by the Lord while both partners of the marriage are alive; death alone severs the marriage bond for such. If a husband leaves his wife he also must remain unmarried.

1 Cor.7:12,13

Here Paul gives advice again, not the Lord. In the progress of the gospel it has often happened that a husband was saved, but not his wife, and sometimes it was the wife who was saved, but not the husband. If the unsaved partner of marriage was content to dwell with the saved partner, then the saved partner was not to leave the unsaved.

1 Cor.7:14

Many interpretations have been attempted as to the meaning of the word sanctified (Gk. hagiazo, to separate, to set apart) as applied to the husband and wife, and holy (Gk. hagios, sanctified or set apart) as applied to the children. Hagiazo here is in the perfect tense, which shows that a past act is indicated, the effect of which remains. The past act was that of the marriage of this pair, when the husband set apart his wife from all others of womankind to be to him what no other woman could lawfully be. Similarly, the wife set apart her husband to be to her what no other man could lawfully be. Hence the ordinance of marriage sanctified each to the other. It did not sanctify them in any sense toward God. The bond of marriage remains, even though one of the parties becomes a believer. It is well, I think, to remember, that marriage is a thing that belongs to the human family, and to no other species of creature, whether heavenly or earthly.

When marriage is contracted the original law obtains that man and woman so joined become one flesh and are to remain so during their lifetime. Within this union the procreation of the human race was to take place. Had marriage not taken place, then the children would have been regarded as unclean, illegitimate, born out of wedlock, but being born in wedlock, they are holy, being born within a sanctified union. As to the sanctification which results from the acceptance of Christ by faith through the gospel, the children of Christian parents are no more sanctified than the children of unbelieving parents. The children of saints are not saints until they believe in Christ, and in no sense does baptism bring such on to Christian ground, as some allege.

1 Cor.7:15,16

If the unbelieving departed they were to be allowed to go, the brother or sister was not to be in bondage in such an eventuality. It was an act of God that had made the difference between them. But if this happened, the same condition existed as laid down in verse 11, that there could be no remarriage by the believing partner while the other was alive. God called His saints in peace, and they were to avoid all strife. The object of the believing wife or husband was to be the salvation of the other, and that would call for a Christ-like spirit, by which the unbelieving could be shown the excellencies of that life which those who receive the grace of God should show (1 Pet.3:1-4).

1 Cor.7:17

Here we have the matter of a man's gift referred to again (verse 7). As God has divided to each, so is to be the behaviour of each. God's calling is according to his gift. Such was Paul's teaching in all the churches. One teaching brought similar results.

1 Cor.7:18,19

In Gal.6:15, Paul says, "For neither is circumcision anything, nor uncircumcision, but a new creature." He also shows that should a man that is a believer receive circumcision, to perfect the work of salvation, he is a debtor to keep the whole law (Gal.5: 3). Believers were to regard the rite of circumcision as nothing in this dispensation, the chief matters were becoming a new creature in Christ and the keeping of the commandments afterwards. The believer has been circumcised in the circumcision of Christ, in the putting off of the body of the flesh (Col.2:11).

1 Cor.7:20,21,22,23,24

Difficulties existed in things religious, as between the circumcision and the uncircumcision, and in social status in slaves and freemen, among the early disciples. There was to be no rising or scramble among those who were slaves to be free, but if they could become free, they were to use it rather. Some have said that Paul's meaning in the words "use it rather," is, and the Greek requires it, "remain in slavery," rather than be free, which seems to be an extraordinary interpretation. Slaves were to care nothing for their bondage, for they were the Lord's freedmen. Such as were called being free were to regard themselves as the Lord's slaves, bought by His precious blood. Consequently, as being the Lord's by right of purchase, they were not to sell themselves and to become bondservants of men. Each was to abide with God in the calling wherein he was called.

1 Cor.7:25,26

Paul had received no commandment from the Lord on the subject with which he treats. In verse 26 he evidently has virgins, male or female, before his mind, and he reasons from the standpoint of "the present distress," or the existing necessity. It is not clear what this necessity was, but it may be that necessity connected with the work of God which lay so heavily on the apostle's heart. Marriage and family rearing call for much time, which, perhaps, Paul saw could be used in the cause of Christ. Paul uses the Greek word anthropos, a word similar in meaning to "mankind," which applies to both men and women.

1 Cor.7:27,28

Paul's opinion is that a believer is not to seek a change; if bound to a wife in marriage, he is not to seek to be loosed, and if he is loosed from a wife (whether he means that the person never married or that his wife had died; how the loosing occurred he does not say), the man is not to seek a wife. But if the man marries he has not sinned, and if the virgin marries she has not sinned. Paul wrote later, that "marriage be had in honour among all" (Heb.13:4). Paul would save the unmarried the troubles in the flesh that marriage brings, both to men and women.

1 Cor.7:29,30

The time or season is shortened, indicative of the brevity of the season which saints are given to be devoted to the service of God. Such as had wives were to be as though they had none, for mere married happiness is not the high aim of the servants of Christ, however pleasant such a life may be, at least in part. Those that wept and those that rejoiced would yet be as though these had not been their experiences, and such as possessed would in time be as though they had nothing. Such experiences in life are fleeting like clouds on an April day. Seasons are ever changing in this brief earthly life. The Lord taught His disciples to hate their life in this world (Lk.14:26; Jn 12:25).

1 Cor.7:31

The believer being a pilgrim in this world is to use the world, but not use it to the full. He is to remember how short his stay is here, and to use the things of the world as a sojurner would do. Further, with the world itself there is no permanency, its fashion passeth away. It seems at one moment as something beautiful and attractive as a flower, again it withers and dies and is gone. So its fashion changes and perishes. The wise man said of it, "Vanity of vanities, all is vanity" (Eccles.1:2).

1 Cor.7:32,33

The Lord in the parable of the sower spoke of the seed that fell among thorns, that "the care of the world, and the deceitfulness of riches, choke the word, and he becometh unfruitful" (Matt.13:22). Paul says here that he would have the Corinthians free from cares, or distractions, from having a divided mind. He says that the unmarried is careful for the things of the Lord, that he may please the Lord, but the married is careful for the things of the world, that he may please his wife. This view which Paul gives colours all he says on the subject of marriage. The things of the Lord were to Paul his very life; they were his sole interest. He was a man of singleness of purpose and all his energies flowed in one channel.

1 Cor.7:34,35

Here Paul draws a difference between the wife and the virgin. The virgin is careful for the things of the Lord, that she may please Him, but the wife is careful for the things of the world, that she may please her husband. This makes a very wide difference. The virgin may be holy (set apart for the Lord) both in body and spirit. Paul says that he says this for their profit, not as casting a noose for their feet, for were someone to follow this course who had not the gift of celibacy it might be fatal. Paul's object was that the saints might attend upon the Lord without distraction.

1 Cor.7:36,37,38

We have now come to what may be the most difficult part of this chapter. The Greek word parthenos, virgin, that is, a woman who has not known man, or a male virgin, is used in the New Testament fourteen times. Parthenia, virginity, is used only once (Lk.2:36). Parthenos, according to Liddell and Scott, besides being used as a noun, is used as an adjective in Greek literature, but it is not used as an adjective in the New Testament. In verses 36 and 37 above, it will be seen that daughter is in italics, showing that there is no word for "daughter" in the Greek. The AV/KJV is correct in omitting "daughter".

Parthenia, virginity, is not found in this chapter, it is invariably parthenos, virgin; yet Mr. Darby and the Englishman's Greek New Testament render parthenos as virginity in verses 36 and 37: I am not disposed to follow their rendering of parthenos as though it were parthenia. I think that the AV/KJV and RV give the correct meaning of the passage by rendering Parthenos as virgin in each occurrence of the word. The verses above deal with a father and his virgin, that is, his virgin daughter. The father has to judge which course is best for his daughter, whether to give her in marriage or to keep her with himself. It may sound rather strange in our ears in modern times, that a father had so much power as to decide the matter of his daughter's future, whether she should marry or not.

But in Paul's days the father evidently had the right of decision as to his daughter whether she should marry or not. The words, "Let him do what he will; he sinneth not," refer to the father, and not to the prospective husband, as though Paul was giving licence for irregular conduct. The father who gave his daughter in marriage did not sin, nor did the young people who married sin, but Paul says that the father who gives his virgin in marriage doeth well, but he who giveth her not in marriage doeth better. This view of Paul's runs throughout the whole paragraph, in which he gives his own judgement, but not the commandment of the Lord.

1 Cor.7:39,40

Here Paul is again giving instruction to believers relative to the marriage bond, that it continues during the lifetime of the contracting parties. If a woman's husband dies, then she is free to be married to whom she will, but her will is to be regulated by the Lord's will, for she is to marry "only in the Lord." "In the Lord" means to be subject to His will within the sphere where His will obtains. It is not equivalent to being "in Christ", which term includes all who are new creatures in Him (2 Cor.5,17), and are members of His Body (1 Cor.12:12,13; Rom.12:5). Paul reaffirms to the woman what he said to the man who was loosed from a wife, that he was not to seek a wife (verse 27). He says that the widow will be happier if she remains unmarried. In giving his counsel to men and women virgins, widowers and widows, he is not giving the Lord's commandment, but as a faithful servant of the Lord, he draws the line between the higher life and that wherein the things of the world come in to cause distraction. In what he had written Paul says that he thought he had the Spirit of God guiding him in what he wrote.

I should like to say before I conclude this chapter, that there is no question but that this whole chapter is part of the inspired Scriptures, for the Spirit caused him to write thus to give his considered judgement on an important matter, that of marriage. He shows the claims of the higher life of devotion to the Lord and to His work.

COMMENTARY ON 1 CORINTHIANS 8

1 Cor.8:1,2,3

In this chapter Paul passes on to the subject of idolatry and things sacrificed to idols. It seems to be the natural sequence of events, that where man has not the knowledge of the true God he drifts into idolatry. Covetousness is idolatry (Col.3:5), which is the devotion of one's being to material and earthly things, and this leads on to gross forms of idolatry. The Greek word eidololatreia comes from eidolon, an idol, and latreia, service or worship, eidolon is derived from eido, to see. In connexion with idolatry Paul says that human knowledge "puffeth up." No doubt, as covetousness is the essential spirit of idolatry, and with this pride walks hand in hand, for it adds to man's natural pride to choose and serve his own god. Here we see the perversion which sin has wrought in the human heart.

Athens with all its philosophy and human wisdom did not disentangle itself from idolatry. Pride and idolatry walked together there well pleased with each other's company. Paul says that if a man thinketh that he knoweth anything (that is, in the realm of the knowledge of God and His ways), he knoweth not yet as he ought to know; but, he adds, "if any man loveth God, the same is known of Him." Herein lies the great and immeasurable distance between idolatry and the knowledge of God. Idolatry, that heartless, loveless, sterile, cold, and oftentimes intensely cruel thing, knows nothing of love which characterizes the knowledge of God. The true God is a Lover, and not merely a Lover, He is Love, essential Love in His Being. "He that loveth not knoweth not God; for God is Love" (1 Jn 4:8,9:10).

His love is revealed to us in the sending of His Son, and in His Son's atoning death on the cross. His love begets love in the believer's heart.

Love, therefore, is the outstanding difference between the loveless, lifeless idol, and the living and true God, the loving Father of all believers. The present grasping of men of the world after materialism, for the world is full of materialism, will reach its climax in the bringing into existence of the great and opulent city of Babylon, as described in Rev. 17, 18, a city great and rich, but whose greatness and riches shall perish at the hands of God and man. It will nevertheless lead on to the worship of the (wild) beast, the worst form of idolatry which the world has ever seen or will ever see.

1 Cor. 8:4,5,6

An idol is nothing in the world; though it should be made of gold and studded all over with precious stones, it is a piece of inanimate material which can neither hear nor see, nor can it think, speak or walk. Whatever it represented, Jupiter or Zeus, or any other supposed deity, these had no existence whatever, but were imaginary gods, the thought of which demons projected into the minds of men to turn them from the true God. There is one God and one God only, the Divine and Holy Trinity, the Father and the Son and the Holy Spirit; these three Persons are one God. Men deluded by Satan and his hosts of wickedness peopled the heavens with gods of all sorts, for example, Venus, the goddess of love or rather lust, Bacchus, the god of the drunkard, and so on; there were gods many and lords many, but all myths. To us there is one God, the Father, the eternal Father of the eternal Son.

That Jesus Christ is said to be the one Lord in no way detracts from the fact that He is truly and fully God. It is clearly stated, in Jn 1:1, that He, "the Word, was God." What we need to recognize in our time and until the time when He shall deliver up the kingdom to God, even the Father, is that the Lord has been given authority over all in heaven and earth, save only Deity, and in His mediatorial work He is Lord of all (Matt. 28:18; 11:27; Jn 13:3; 1 Cor. 15:24-28).

When His mediatorial work is completed, then the Son shall hand back to the Father the authority which He gave to Him, then things shall return to what they were before the entrance of sin, and God – Father, Son and Holy Spirit – shall be all in all. The Lord Jesus must reign until He has put all things under His feet, and has finally abolished death, which will be cast into the lake of fire. Besides having had all authority given to Him, He has been made High Priest; He who is God has graciously taken the office of High Priest in order that we may worship God in spirit and truth (Jn 4: 23; Heb.5:5-10). The order in which we approach to God the Father in prayer and praise is in the Spirit (Eph.2:18; 5:20, 6: 18; Phil.3:3), through the Son (Eph.2:18; Heb.13: 15; 1 Pet.2:5). All things are of (Gk. ek out of) the Father and we unto (Gk. eis, into) Him, and all things are through (Gk. dia, through, as the channel or cause) the Son, the Lord Jesus, and we through (dia) Him.

1 Cor.8:7,8

All men had not the knowledge of God as outlined by the apostle in the previous verses. God is the Giver of all through His Son, but many, many, even some of the saints in Corinth evidently, associated the meat with the idol, as though a dumb idol could either give or receive anything. The meat which was God's gift through Jesus Christ was not changed in its quality, even though it had been offered to an idol. But where believers ate such meat as of a thing sacrificed to an idol their conscience, being weak, was defiled, for they had been brought up to idol worship. Eating played a great part in idolatry. It also played a large part in the ceremonial life of the children of Israel. Eating does not commend men to God, nor yet if they do not eat are they the better through abstinence. The eating that brings lasting benefits is the eating by faith (Jn 6:35,40,47,51,54). Faith is the mouth of the soul. But we are neither the better nor the worse spiritually if we eat or do not eat. Physically we are better if we eat, but to be strong in the flesh does not mean that we shall be strong in faith.

1 Cor.8:9,10

The saints in Corinth were to take heed lest the liberty (Gk. exousia, which means authority, which they had through the apostle's teaching) they enjoyed in regard to the eating of meats should become a stumbling-block to those who were weak as to their conscience. Should a saint who had knowledge be seen, by one who was weak, sitting eating in an idol's temple, would not the weak person be emboldened to do likewise, not being able to distinguish between the Divine Giver of the meat to whom alone thanks were due, and the idol to which it had been offered? Thus in the eating of things which had been sacrificed to an idol the weak brother's conscience is defiled.

1 Cor.8:11,12,13

Here is seen the effect that knowledge, through unwise action, may destroy a brother for whom Christ died. "Perisheth," in verse 11, is the same word as "perish" in Jn 3:16, but it has not the same meaning. In Jn it means the utter loss of the unbeliever in eternal woe, here it means the loss of the believer's life in service for God. It is evident from what Paul says, that a believer may act with a perfectly good conscience toward God, yet if his acting is harmful to the sincere yet weak conscience of another, and so wounding the other's conscience, he sins against the brethren, and thus sins against Christ. The importance of such a consideration is not always appreciated. The knowledgeable believer may be inclined to act without due regard for the conscientious feeling of others. Paul's attitude in the light of the well-being of others is to be admired and copied, that if his meat-eating were to cause his brother to stumble, he would eat no flesh for evermore.

COMMENTARY ON 1 CORINTHIANS 9

1 Cor.9:1,2,3

Whilst in the former chapter he shows that his actions in regard to eating were dependent upon the spiritual growth and attainment of his brethren, that he did all for their profit, he shows in this chapter that in his apostleship he was quite independent of men in their attitude to him. He was a free man, an apostle of the Lord who was under his Divine Master's complete control. Indeed, he had received his apostleship directly from the Lord, for he had seen Him. The Corinthians were his work in the Lord, a work which he had carried out in subjection to the Lord. If others might not regard him as an apostle, he should be so regarded by them, for he had come to them as sent by the Lord carrying the glad tidings of the gospel. They were the seal of his apostleship in the Lord. Such was his defence to those who would examine him, as well as what he says afterwards.

1 Cor.9:4,5,6

Was Paul's maintenance not chargeable upon the Corinthians, though he did not exercise his right? Had he not authority to take about a wife who was a sister, like the rest of the apostles and the brethren of the Lord, the natural sons of Joseph and Mary? He particularly mentions Cephas, who was a married man (Matt.8:14). Were Paul and Barnabas to be denied the comforts of married life, to be eunuchs for the kingdom of heaven's sake? (Matt.19:12). Had they also no right to forbear working while they preached the word? The answers to these questions, which must have shamed the Corinthians, are obvious.

1 Cor.9:7

Here Paul uses three illustrations to force home his argument of his right to claim support from the Corinthians, the soldier, the vinedresser, and the shepherd. The soldier is maintained by the king or rulers of his country; the husbandman eats the fruit of his labours; and the shepherd partakes of the milk of the flock. All were maintained in and by their several occupations, but, alas, the carnal Corinthians took little or no thought for the apostle and his needs, though they owed him much.

1 Cor.9:8,9,10

Paul does not draw his illustrations from men, but from the law, and from nature's school. First he shows that when the ox was labouring for its master, and there was abundance of food beneath its feet, it must not be prohibited from eating as it went round and round in the threshing floor. It must not be muzzled. It must be allowed to share in the good of its labours. But there was a deeper meaning than oxen in the law, God had also human labourers in view, and so Paul applies the parable to himself and his fellow-labourers. The Corinthians put the parsimonious muzzle on Paul and his fellows, causing them to work with their own hands for their maintenance. Such niggardliness is to their abiding dishonour. Besides the parable about the ox, Paul cites the ploughman and him that thresheth as instances of the hope of the labourer of partaking of the fruit of his toil.

1 Cor.9:11,12

Paul had sowed the seed of the gospel and the truth for believers in their hearts, and God had caused it to grow, but where was the fruit? Was there to be no response for the much labour which had been expended upon them? The Corinthians seemed to minister to the need of others to whom they were less indebted than to Paul. But in spite of such unworthy treatment Paul bore it all. He said, "We bear all things," though, no doubt, the attitude of the Corinthians was hard to bear, and besides, he bore many other afflictions in silence. His object in all this was to cause no hindrance to the gospel of Christ.

1 Cor.9:13,14

Paul here alludes to the Aaronic priesthood in the service of the temple and the altar. Whatever their service was, they had their portion with that with which their service lay. These things are evident from even a cursory reading of Leviticus. From this Paul draws his conclusion, that such as proclaim the gospel should live of the gospel.

1 Cor.9:15,16

Paul did not use his right to live of the gospel, and he did not write thus that the Corinthians should minister to his necessities. There is a touch of censure in what he says, that it were better for him to die rather than that any should make his boasting void. He would continue to do as he had done, even to work with his own hands. His mission was to preach the gospel, and of that he had nothing to glory; it was a matter of necessity, for woe to him if he failed in this, the work which the Lord had given him to do.

1 Cor.9:17,18

It was as a free man in the exercise of his own will that Paul preached the gospel; then, in that case, he had a reward; but if not of his own will, but according to the will of Another, he had a stewardship intrusted to him, and to his Master, he was accountable. "What is our hope, or joy, or crown of glorying? Are not even ye, before our Lord Jesus at His coming? For ye are our glory and our joy"! (1 Thess.2:19,20). He likewise called the Philippians, "my joy and crown" (4:1).

1 Cor.9:19,20

Paul was a free man, yet he brought himself into slavery to the prejudices of men to gain (Gk. kerdos, gain or profit) the more. To the Jews he became as a Jew to gain Jews. This accounts for his circumcising Timothy (Acts 16:3). He did it, we are told, "because of the Jews that were in those parts." It explains, in part, his act, in Acts 21:17-26, when, because of Jewish prejudices, lest what was untruthfully reported of him should hinder and mar God's work, he purified himself in the temple with the four men who had a vow upon them. Though Paul was a Jew by race, he was not a Jew according to their formal religion, though he adapted himself to meet their weakness for formality in order to gain them. Likewise to those who were under law, his actions toward them were such as to gain them also, though he was not under the law himself. Had he acted as Gentiles did, he would have closed the door to the entrance of the gospel among them. His overruling consideration in all his actions was to gain men for Christ.

1 Cor.9:21,22,23

As one without law he spoke to the philosophers at Athens. In his address he made no reference directly to the Old Testament, but quoted one of their own poets. How differently he spoke to the Jews in the synagogue in Antioch of Pisidia, in Acts 13:13-43! His address there is full of references to the Scriptures. How able he was to meet those who were without law on their own ground! Paul himself was not without law, for he was under law to Christ, not under the law of Moses. To the weak in conscience he so acted as not to offend their prejudices; he adapted himself in such a way so that he might gain them with the gospel. He was so efficient in his presentation of Christ, that if they were offended, they were offended at Christ, not with the apostle's behaviour.

It may well be that men are not offended with Christ, but offended with the character and behaviour of those who seek to speak of Him.

He did all things for the gospel's sake, that he might be a joint partaker thereof. Long years after Paul had gone to rest his gospel message bore abundant fruit. It was his words, in Rom.1, that "the just shall live by faith" that illuminated the soul of Luther. It was hearing the reading of the commentary of Luther on the epistle to the Romans that enlightened John Wesley. Paul's words have flowed out like streams in the desert to many weary travellers, bringing life and enlightenment. So will it be until time is no more.

1 Cor.9:24,25

Paul here alludes to the race and the prize. The life of the Christian is compared here both to a race and a fight, as it is elsewhere in the New Testament. He counsels the Cor.so to run as to obtain the prize. How often Christians are like divers (with boots of lead) rather than runners! Paul speaks of the temperance of the athlete. He allows himself only what will keep his body nourished with essential food so that it may be in prime condition for the contest. The object in it all is only a corruptible crown. One phase of the fruit of the Spirit in the Christian is temperance (Gal.5:23); this is essential if we are to obtain an incorruptible crown. The Christian must cut down on non-essentials. If he would be a winner he must shed many things which others who have not their eye on the goal think that they can safely allow themselves. Think of Solomon who kept nothing from himself of carnal enjoyment (Eccles.2:1-11), but how did it end with him? His end, for so wise a man, is one of the saddest (1 Kgs.11:1-8). He fed the flesh and at the last the flesh devoured him.

1 Cor.9:26,27

Paul was a temperate runner; there was no uncertainty in his running. Everything unnecessary was laid aside. Bodily appetites were suppressed. In his boxing he did not beat the air. He so boxed as to bruise his body and bring it into bondage. His body was his instrument in which he did God's will, not his master. His type of mind naturally was that, when he espoused a cause, he was whole-hearted in it. This is seen in his educational pursuits, and His advancement in youth among the Jewish leaders. Then, when his mind was sanctified by the Spirit, he pursued the Lord's work with a diligence which, I think, had never been surpassed by any mere man. His reason for keeping under the appetites of the body was, lest by any means, after he had preached to others, he himself should be rejected. Rejected is from the Greek word adokimos, which means disapproved, rejected, one that is useless, in AV/KJV it is rendered by "a castaway". This does not mean that a saved person can become a lost soul again, but it shows what a servant of Christ may become as to his service. Paul is dealing with service and reward, not with the gift of salvation. Salvation and eternal life are gifts, not rewards.

COMMENTARY ON 1 CORINTHIANS 10

1 Cor.10:1,2

Paul now passes from the thought of the athletes, the games and the prizes, the winners and those rejected, to Israel in the wilderness and to the time of their testing. God has ever since the time of the garden of Eden put man under a test. Job said in the time of his testing, "When He hath tried me, I shall come forth as gold" (Job 23:10). The first test for Israel after they had been delivered from Egypt was at the Red Sea where they were all baptized unto (Gk. eis into) Moses (see Rom.6:3), who was their new ruler. Pharaoh's yoke had been broken from off their neck. Many, many of God's children have failed in this first step of the disciple pathway, that of baptism, and have proved themselves useless in the path of the subjection and obedience to the Lord. In Israel's case they were all baptized unto Moses in the cloud and in the sea (1 Cor.10:2).

1 Cor.10:3,4

As at the Red Sea Israel murmured against Moses saying, "Because there were no graves in Egypt, hast thou taken us away to die in the wilderness? wherefore hast thou dealt thus with us, to bring us forth out of Egypt?" They murmured in the wilderness of Sin at the time of the giving of the manna. They said, "Would that we had died by the hand of the LORD in the land of Egypt, when we sat by the flesh pots, when we did eat bread to the full; for ye have brought us forth into this wilderness, to kill this whole assembly with hunger." Then when they came to Rephidim, when there was no water for the people to drink, we have the worst case of murmuring, indeed the camp had reached a state of rebellion, for "Moses cried unto the LORD, saying, What shall I do unto this people? they be almost ready to stone me?"

This bitter experience the LORD never forgot, for they questioned, "Is the LORD among us, or not?" The bitter memory of that experience lingered with the LORD and with David, as we read in Ps.95:7-11: "To-day, Oh that ye would hear His voice! Harden not your heart, as at Meribah, As in the day of Massah in the wilderness: When your fathers tempted Me, Proved Me, and saw My work. Forty years long was I grieved with that generation, And said, It is a people that do err in their heart, And they have not known My ways: Wherefore I sware in My wrath, That they should not enter into My rest."

Let the reader who is in God's house today ponder well the words of Heb.3:5-19, where we have a similar line of truth as to the tests that God puts His saints through. Similarly, let such as are facing the truth of divine separation and of the associated truth of the house of God consider well and gravely the responsibility of hearing and responding to the voice of God. Much, yea, very much, will depend on how such stand the test of obedience to God. Note that the rest is God's rest, which is in His house today. See Acts 7:49: Israel ate the manna for forty years. At the smiting of the rock by Moses, God "opened the rock, and waters gushed out" (Ps.105:41). We are told that the rock was a rock of flint (Deut.8:15), and flint naturally when struck by steel gives forth fire, but this one when struck by Moses' almond rod gave forth water in abundance. It went ill with Moses for their sake in the wilderness of Zin, for there that meek man was so exasperated by Israel that he rebelled against the Lord. He smote the Rock instead of speaking to it, and for this he was not allowed to enter the land of Canaan (Num.20:1-13).

Though Israel drank of the Rock which followed them, which was Christ, yet Ps.78:25 speaks of rocks, "He clave rocks in the wilderness, And gave them drink abundantly as out of the depths." The giving of water being a miracle of grace, we cannot pursue the matter to finality. We must accept what God says about it, that Christ as the water-giving

Rock followed Israel through the wilderness, and that the Rock should never have been struck but once.

1 Cor.10:5

Paul deals, in Heb.3 and Heb.4, with this matter of the overthrow of all the numbered men of the twelve tribes, who were numbered from twenty years and upward at Sinai, when they gave the half shekel in silver of the atonement money. This is a very important line of truth for those in the house of God, as to the matter of the falling away from the living God, the God of the house of God. There can be no falling away from grace as to the matter of salvation, for once a person is saved from hell, that person is saved with eternal salvation of which Christ is the Author. But as surely as such a person cannot fall away and be lost, so surely it is that saved people who are in God's house can fall away and their lives of service for God can be lost, and their crown of reward or other reward lost at the judgement-seat of Christ. We commend for consideration this matter of the numbering of Israel, their atonement by atonement money, the use to which the money was put, and the consequences of the rebellion of the tribes at Kadesh-barnea (Ex.30:11-16, Ex.38:25-28; Num.13,14; Heb.3,4).

1 Cor.10:6,7,8,9,10

The events which Paul enumerates here are examples (Gk. tupos, a mark, type or figure) to be avoided. In these cases we are to shun the examples shown here in Israel. Firstly, they despised the manna, and lusted for Egypt's savouries, its fish, leeks, onions, garlick, its cucumbers and melons, and said, "Our soul is dried away; there is nothing at all: we have nought save this manna to look to" (Num.11:5,6). It is sad when the believer finds little pleasure in the reading of the Scriptures and turns to the world's savoury, or unsavoury, novel reading. Soon the desire for Christ will disappear also. This is the way to take a short-cut to spiritual death. Then Israel became idolaters in the matter of the golden calf. "Play," Ex.32:6, means to play, sport, jest, to laugh repeatedly, to play as a boy.

It is sad to think that a people redeemed from Egypt's slavery but a few months before should sink to such depths as to make idolatry a matter of eating and drinking and revelry. John says, "My little children, guard yourselves from idols" (1 Jn 5:21). Then amongst these examples fornication lifts its ugly head; it is ever the companion of idolatry. The teaching of Balaam led many like an ox to the slaughter. The daughters of Moab were let loose amongst the Israelites and in their lust the men of Israel joined themselves to Baal-worship. In Num.25:1-9, we read that 24,000 died of the plague at that time; of these Paul says that 23,000 fell in one day. Whilst Balaam could not get God to turn against Israel, his teaching turned many men of Israel from God.

In Num.21:4-9 we are told how Israel tempted God. It says that they were much discouraged because of the way. "Discouraged" means shortened, that is, impatient, prone to anger. Then they spoke against God and against Moses, and said, "Wherefore have ye brought us up out of Egypt to die in the wilderness? for there is no bread, and there is no water; and our soul loatheth this light (despicable or vile) bread." Their tempers were short and they perished by the fiery serpents. Though the story describes an evil day in Israel's history, yet the narrative by being touched by the Lord's hand has perhaps been more blessed in the salvation of sinners than any other in the Old Testament. See Jn 3:14,15: They also murmured and perished by the destroyer. Such was the case in the matter of Korah and his company, and such also was the case with the whole congregation of numbered men who murmured and perished in the wilderness. Murmuring was a besetting sin in Israel in the wilderness.

1 Cor.10:11,12,13

These examples of failure on the part of Israel are held up as warnings to us, having been written for our admonition, which means to put something on the mind which will act as a corrective. We are such as live at "the ends of the ages." It does not seem to me that this is identical with "the end or completion of the age" (Matt.28:20), or "at the end of these days" (Heb.1:1). It seems more in accord with "now once at the end (completion) of the ages hath He been manifested to put away sin by the sacrifice of Himself" (Heb.9:26). It would seem that past ages will be completed by the mediatorial work of the Lord. That will be when at the great white throne judgement He finally deals with men and casts death and hell into the lake of fire and also all that are not written in the book of life. When this is accomplished He will deliver up the kingdom to God even the Father, and God will be all in all, that is God the Father, the Son, and the Holy Spirit, and things shall return into the channel in which they flowed before the entrance of sin (1 Cor.15:24-28).

Then will come into view the eternal order of things in a new heaven and a new earth. This new order will find its base in the reconciling work of the Lord; peace will flow for ever from the blood of His cross (Col.1:20). In this our day of testing we are never free from the fear that we may fail in the test, hence the warning of the apostle, that he that thinketh he standeth is to take heed lest he fall; and it is to be observed that the apostle uses the words "thinketh he standeth," as though there is no certainty that any one of us is really standing. The temptations which God allows to come upon us are all bearable. It is like the old proverbial saying, that "He tempers the wind to the shorn lamb." His gracious provision is, that with the temptation He makes the way of escape, and, as Pet. says, "The Lord knoweth how to deliver the godly out of temptation" (2 Pet.2:9). "The prize, the prize secure! The wrestler nearly fell; Bare all he could endure, And bare not always well; But he may smile at troubles gone Who has the victor-garland on."

1 Cor.10:14,15,16,17

As we are to "flee fornication" (1 Cor.6:18), so are we to "flee from idolatry." The words which follow this exhortation were written to intelligent ones, hence they are words not easy to be understood, but we shall endeavour to glean somewhat of their meaning, even though we may fail in clarity of exposition. First of all we may ask, Why is the blood mentioned before the body? The order of words in speaking of man in his natural state, is to speak of him as flesh and blood (Matt.16:17; Gal.1:16; Eph.6:12; 1 Cor.15:50), but when referring to the incarnation the order is reversed in Heb.2:14, RVM.: "Since then the children are sharers in blood and flesh, He also Himself in like manner partook of the same." The blood of Christ speaks of the death of Christ. In the past the death of the peace offering was the base of communion. The peace offering was the fellowship offering. It brought God and men together in that they each shared a part of the peace offering.

God's part was the blood and the kidneys with the fat or suet that covered the inwards. These came to the altar. The priest and the priestly family got the wave breast and the heave thigh, and the offerer the rest of the offering, and of this every one that was clean could eat. See Leviticus, chapter 3, and chapter 7:11-38: God's portion came first in the sprinkling of the blood of the peace offering, then the burning of the fat, and then came the priest's portions, and then the offerer's. See 1 Sam.2:12-17: What this portion of Paul's epistle is now dealing with is communion, and in that matter the blood of Christ comes first, for, as we have said, blood shedding is the base of communion.

We now ask a further question, Do the words of verses 16,17 refer to the ordinary eating of food by believers, or do they refer to the eating in communion at the breaking of bread in the Lord's remembrance on Lord's day? Our view is that it is that communion in the partaking of the loaf and the cup on the Lord's day and not an ordinary meal. Indeed this portion deals with special eating cited by the apostle in each case: (1) the eating in which we partake of one bread or loaf; (2) the eating in

Israel by those who ate of the sacrifices and ate in communion with the altar; and (3) the eating of the Gentiles who ate of the sacrifices which had been sacrificed to demons in idol worship. In each case, therefore, it is not the ordinary eating of food, but the eating in communion of an extraordinary kind. Concerning the cup of blessing (Eulogia, blessing, praise) which we bless (Gk. eulogeo, means, literally, to speak well of, hence to praise or give thanks), bless here is in the same sense as in 1 Cor.14:16, also Matt.26:26 ("it" in the AV/KJV in the latter scripture is in italics and should not appear, as there is no word for it in the Greek). Bless means the same as to give thanks. See also Jas.3:9, etc.

The word bless does not mean that something is imparted to the loaf and the cup, involving a change of substance, as the Romish priests profess to change them, when they say in Latin, "This is My body," and "This is My blood," in their heresy of transubstantiation. "The cup of blessing," Paul says, "is a communion of the blood of Christ." Communion (Gk. koinonia) means joint-participation, fellowship, communion. This communion can be enjoyed only by those who are in union with Christ, in other words, by saved persons. Communion should never be confused with union, with the individual reception of Christ by a personal faith in Him. There is no communion in that act. In that act of faith the believing sinner eats of the Lord's flesh and drinks of His blood (Jn 6:54), and in consequence has eternal life; it is the same as believing in Him, by which the believer has eternal life (Jn 6:47). The teaching of Jn 6 should never be confused with communion in the Lord's remembrance. These things are entirely apart and different, though of course the church of Rome confuses them in the mass to her financial advantage in her commercialized religion. "We bless," and "we break," show joint action by the many, though it is done by one brother who acts for the whole.

Having dealt with the thought of communion of the blood and the body of Christ in verse 16, Paul proceeds to something different in verse 17, to the union of saints, who are now viewed as one bread or loaf, and those that are many are not only one loaf, but they are one Body, and the reason given is that they partake of (Gk. ek, out of) one loaf. Dr. Young in his critical comments gives a literal rendering of the verse, which is almost identical with what he gives in his literal translation of the Scriptures: "Because one loaf, one Body, are we the many, for we all partake of one loaf," which is practically the same as in the Englishman's Greek New Testament, though there is a slight alteration in the position of the words.

The question that at once arises is, Do the many become one Body, that is the Body of Christ, the Church, by eating in communion the symbols of the body and blood of Christ in the bread and wine on the Lord's day? The answer must be, No. We become members of that one Body when we believe on Christ and are baptized in one Spirit into that one Body (1 Cor.12:13). It must be conceded that many, many of the members of Christ do not eat in communion at all. The members of that Body are scattered in almost all the sects in Christendom, and there exists no communion between them. My view of the verse is, that the one loaf of which the many partake is of the body of Christ by faith, that is His own body, not His Body, the Church. In consequence of this partaking of Christ by faith, we who are many are one loaf, one Body. It will therefore in this interpretation of these verses be seen that the word loaf or bread signifies three things in verses 16 and 17: (1) In verse 16 it refers to the loaf of the Lord's remembrance (1 Cor.11:23, 24); (2) it refers to the saints, "we, who are many, are one loaf, one Body," and (3) the actual body (or Person) of Christ, of which all believers partake and so become one Body in Him.

1 Cor.10:18

Here is another communion of Israel after the flesh, in which those that ate the sacrifices were joint-partakers with the altar. Both priests and people who ate of the sacrifice of peace offerings ate in communion with the altar. The altar portion was God's portion of the offering made by fire.

1 Cor.10:19,20

An idol was nothing, nor what was sacrificed to it, save that it was God's food for man put to a wrong use. An idol was often the representation of a god that had no existence; they were mere figments of the minds of men deceived by the devil and his demons. What was the evil in idolatry? It was this, that the things that the Gentiles sacrificed, they sacrificed them to demons and not to God. The view of the Greeks and others of old was that men could not reach God except through demons, and contrariwise, God could not reach men save through demons. This idea of demon mediators shows how firmly established the devil was in the thoughts of men. Demons, according to the Greek idea, were petty gods. Spiritism spreads its evil influence in most ancient nations, and it still prevails in many quarters today.

The Roman Catholic Church with its teaching of the virgin Mary and the saints as mediators with the Father and the Son is a form of the ancient evil. This whole paragraph, from verses 14 to 22, has to do with fleeing from idolatry, and the matter of communion. Thus Paul says, "I would not that ye should have communion with demons." To eat meat as having been sacrificed to an idol was to have communion with demons, for lurking behind the idol were these evil spirits.

1 Cor.10:21,22

Here Paul shows the incompatibility of seeking to join the cup of the Lord and the cup of demons. The cup of the Lord is the same as the cup of blessing which we bless (verse 16). Also, he says, that it is impossible to partake of the table of the Lord, which is implied in the bread or loaf which we break (verse 16), and the table of demons, in sharing in the sacrifice to an idol. Nowhere do we read of that much travestied statement, "the Father's table," the table deluded people say is for all His children. Such an idea is not found in the New Testament. The Lord's Remembrance should be kept in a church of God and nowhere else. Nowhere is it contemplated that the breaking of the bread is the privilege of God's children whether they are divinely gathered or not, or whether their condition morally and spiritually is as it ought to be.

We know that there are many sins possible of being committed by born-again people which would preclude them from sharing in the breaking of the bread, so the Lord's table cannot be the Father's table for all His children unconditionally. Paul asks, "What agreement hath a temple of God (a church of God) with idols?" (2 Cor.6:16). The answer is, None at all! Demons and the Lord cannot be joined together. Of old Israel provoked the LORD to jealousy in the worship of the golden calf (Ex.32), which almost led to their destruction, but for the pleading of Moses. Moses said, "The LORD thy God is a devouring fire, a jealous God" (Deut.4:24, 5: 9). Even so is our God (Heb.12:29).

1 Cor.10:23,24

Here Paul repeats what he said in chapter 6:12 about Christian liberty, that all things are lawful, but all things are not expedient. He is not dealing with things that are definitely unlawful and in their nature sinful. The Christian is not under a restrictive code of – Do not do this, and, do not do that. His actions are to be directed by love, love to God and love to his neighbour. The legal code of the law of Moses and of all the Old Testament which the Lord summed up in few words clears up the matter of the Christian's freedom of action, "All things therefore whatsoever ye would that men should do unto you, even so do ye also unto them: for this is the law and the prophets" (Matt.7:12). This is the substance of what Paul says, "Let no man seek his own, but each his neighbour's good." Hence we are to abandon things which we could do quite lawfully, if we find that they would be harmful to our neighbour. His edification should be our aim.

1 Cor.10:25,26

Meat that was sold in a market, as the flesh of the sacrifices in the idol's temple often was, was to be eaten without question being raised as to whence it had come, for conscience sake, of the believer who bought, the seller, or any other. The earth being the Lord's and the fulness thereof, the meat was His. The fact that it had been put to a wrong use in being offered to an idol had not changed its character or its quality, it was still the Lord's.

1 Cor.10:27,28,29

If a believer were called or bidden by an unbeliever ("to a feast" is not in the Greek), and the believer was disposed to respond to the invitation, he was to eat, asking no question for conscience sake. But if any one should say to him that the meat had been offered to an idol, then he was not to eat, because of the conscience of him that told him this. The believer might be quite clear regarding Paul's teaching, that the meat was the Lord's, though it had been put to the wrong use of being offered to an idol, but for the sake of the conscience of him that showed him that it had been offered to an idol he was not to eat. But Paul asks, "Why is my liberty judged by another conscience?" This is just the question that he is seeking to answer. The believer who had knowledge was to think first of his neighbour's good, as to what effect it would have on his conscience, and not on the satisfying of his own appetite. Herein lies a most important principle in regard to the actions of a believer; he must abstain from things which he may do with a good conscience, if they will be harmful to others.

1 Cor.10:30,31

NOTES ON THE FIRST EPISTLE TO THE CORINTHIANS 75

He asks a further question, that if he by grace thankfully partook of what was the Lord's, for which he had given thanks, why should he be evil spoken of? The question is answered in the next verse, that eating and drinking and all else are to be governed by acting to the glory of God. Acting in a way which is harmful to others is not to the glory of God. The life of the Christian is to be such that men who see it may glorify God in the day of visitation (1 Pet.2:12).

1 Cor.10:32,33

Here is the summing up of true Christian behaviour; it is to be to the profit of others. Some have erroneously concluded that Jews, Greeks (Gentiles, AV/KJV) and the church of God are the three divisions of mankind. What he is saying is about the three divisions of the people, generally speaking, who lived in the city of Corinth. The RV is correct in rendering the original word as Greeks (Gk. hellen, a native of Hellas or Greece), not Gentiles (Gk. ethnos, a nation or people). The church of God was the church of God in Corinth (1 Cor.1:2). There were many churches of God in the apostle's time, and one church of God did not contain all the saints of God on earth. No offence was to be given to any of the inhabitants of Corinth, and, of course, this principle applies to all peoples everywhere. Alas, many believers now-a-days are not in a church of God though, no doubt, they think that they are, because that they are in the Church which is Christ's Body, which is an entirely different thing. There were many churches of God, but only one Body.

There is no contradiction between what Paul says here about pleasing all men for their profit, and what he says, in Gal.1:10, "If I were still pleasing men, I should not be a servant of Christ." In the above verses he is dealing with the conscientious prejudices of men in the matter of eating and drinking, particularly in connection with idolatry, but in Gal. he is dealing with the fundamentals of the gospel, whether salvation is by faith in Christ alone, or whether it is by faith plus the works of the law or any other form of human works. In regard to the latter he did not please men who were out to make a gospel of law and grace, of the work of Christ and the works of men. Because he preached a gospel of grace and faith he suffered much at the hands of men, of the Jews in particular.

COMMENTARY ON 1 CORINTHIANS 11

1 Cor.11:1,2,3

Verse 1 should be joined to chapter 10, as is shown in the RV. In this Paul calls upon the Corinthians to imitate him in his self-denial and self-sacrifice on behalf of others even as he in this matter imitated his Master, Christ. He praised them that they remembered him in all things and that they kept the traditions, the instructions which he had orally delivered to them. Next, Paul deals with headship, that is supremacy. In lordship it is that of authority, the right to command. Headship and lordship are not equivalent terms, though they are often confused. Christ is the Head of the Church which is His Body (Eph.5:23; Col.1:18). Nowhere do we read that He is Lord of the Church. Indeed, it is beyond dispute, that He, the Head, has given no commandments to the Church as such. If He had given to the Church commandments to keep, the Church would have been torn asunder by faction and schism long ago, and it would have been impossible for Him, in the day of His coming, to present the Church to Himself, glorious, without spot, or wrinkle, or any such thing (Eph.5:27).

Had commandments been given by Christ to the Church, the gates of Hades would surely have prevailed. The charter of the Church is, that all therein shall believe that Jesus is the Christ, the Son of the living God (Matt.16:15-18). There is no pope here. "The Church is subject to Christ" (Eph.5:24), but this should not be read that the Church is obedient to Christ, for obedience would imply that commandments had been given by Christ to the Church, and that is not so. Commandments were given by the Lord to His disciples. Discipleship and membership of the Body are two widely different things. The Lord showed what discipleship implied when He said to the Jews which had believed on Him, "If ye abide in My word, then are ye truly My disciples; and ye shall know the truth, and the truth shall make you free" (Jn 8:31,32). Paul says, "The husband is the head of the wife, as Christ also is the Head of the Church" (Eph.5:23). But in consequence of the fall the woman was told, "I will greatly multiply thy sorrow and thy conception; in sorrow thou shalt bring forth children; and thy desire shall be to thy husband, and he shall rule over thee" (Gen.3:16).

The matter of the husband ruling over his wife came in after Eve had sinned in disobeying the command relative to the tree of the knowledge of good and evil. Rule of the husband over his wife was in addition to the headship of the man over the woman. This same thought emerges in the words of Peter, "After this manner aforetime the holy women also, who hoped in God, adorned themselves, being in subjection to their own husbands: as Sarah obeyed Abraham, calling him lord" (1 Pet.3:5,6). We have headship implied in subjection, and also lordship implied in obedience. Paul in Corinthians is not dealing with the headship of the husband over his wife, but the headship of the man over the woman in the assemblings of God's gathered people. The headship of the man and the subjection of the woman does not imply any inferiority on the part of the woman.

She is equal to the man in essence and nature. She is also equal in Christ Jesus, in whom there can be neither male nor female (Gal.3:28). But both in God's assembly and in the domestic sphere the man (Gk. aner, a man, a male person of full age and stature, as opposed to a child or female) is the head of the woman and the husband of the wife. The Head of every man (Gk. aner) is Christ, and the Head of Christ is God. Christ is God and Man, and here He is seen in His mediatorial work in which He is subject to God. It is also true that though Christ the Son of God is equal to the Father (Jn 5:18; Phil.2:6), both in essence and nature, and also in all the attributes of Deity, yet the standing of the Son is one of subjection to the Father (1 Cor.15:28). Subjection does not mean inferiority.

1 Cor.11:4,5

We have pointed out already that what the apostle is writing about is the behaviour of the sexes in the assemblings of God's people, and not in the domestic sphere; the instructions given relative to the women keeping silence in the churches, in 1 Cor.14:34,35, must be borne in mind in the consideration of this matter of praying and prophesying. Paul says, "Let women keep silence in the churches: for it is not permitted unto them to speak; but let them be in subjection, as also saith the law. And if they would learn anything, let them ask their own husbands at home: for it is shameful for a woman to speak in the church." To those who believe that Paul's words are the commandment of the Lord, this scripture cuts out once and for all women speaking publicly, as it says in verse 37.

The Spirit of God would not say that the women are to keep silence in the church, in chapter 14, yet in chapter 11 grant them leave to speak publicly in the church, if they had their head veiled. What do the verses above mean, and what is the practice as based thereon? Does Paul mean that men may sit with their hats on in the church and only take them off when they are going to pray or prophesy? Contrariwise are women contemplated as sitting with their heads unveiled and only veiling their heads when they are going to pray or prophesy? Surely the answers to these questions are No, in both cases.

The correct answer is, I believe, that the church when gathered together is viewed as engaged in praying and prophesying, and should any man present have his head covered during such exercises and while the church is in assembly, which is viewed as a praying and prophesying company, he dishonours Christ his Head, and should a woman be unveiled in church she dishonours man, her head. As to the four virgin daughters of Philip, the evangelist, who prophesied, when, where or how this took place we are not told, but it was neither in a synagogue, for the law forbade it, nor was it in the church, for the teaching of the Lord, as given here by Paul, forbade it, so it would, no doubt, be in the domestic and private life of those virgins.

How and where, "your sons and your daughters shall prophesy" (Acts 2:17) in the future before the great day of the Lord comes, we do not know. By that time the saints of the Church will be with the Lord. It has no application to this dispensation. Paul uses strong words when he says that it would be the same, if a women were unveiled, as if she were shaven.

1 Cor.11:6,7

Paul continues on the theme of the necessity of the woman being veiled, and if not, he says that she should be shorn, and this would be a shame to her. The man is not to have his head veiled, and the reason for this is, that he is the image and glory of God. This carries us back to the creation of man. "God created man in His own image, in the image of God created He him; male and female created He them." He also said, "Let Us make man in Our image, after Our likeness" (Gen.1:26,27). The Hebrew word for image (tselem) means a shadow, a resemblance. The word is used to describe an idol, "an image, likeness (from its shadowing forth": Gesenius). "Likeness" is of somewhat similar meaning (demuwth); it means similitude, likeness, image, appearance. It must not be assumed that when it is said that man was made in the image of God, that this refers to Christ, in incarnation, when He was made in the likeness of men.

The incarnation is the matter in reverse, in that Christ who is the image of the invisible God, took the form of a servant, made in the likeness of men. Man as made by God was made in the shadowy appearance of God and after His likeness. Wherein did this resemblance consist? It could not be in man's physical structure, for God is Spirit and not matter (Jn 4:24). It must be in man's spiritual part, in man's true self. Man's body is simply the tabernacle in which he lives (2 Cor.5:1), which may be dissolved. We get help in this matter of the image of God from Eph.4:24 where we read, "Put on the new man, which after God hath been created in righteousness and holiness of truth." Thus I take it that man as God's image was in holiness and righteousness of truth.

Again we read in Col.3:9,10, "Ye ... have put on the new man, which is being renewed unto knowledge after the image of Him that created him." Thus it seems to me, that while man, as to his spiritual being, was created in God's resemblance, in holiness and righteousness of truth, yet he was capable of being renewed unto knowledge, that is, the knowledge of God and of His ways, and this knowledge was after the image of Him that created him. Solomon tells us "that God made man upright;' but they have sought out many inventions" (Eccles.7:29). God put an upright soul in an upright body. Inventions here means arts or devices, not necessarily mechanical. Men may devise cunning works (Ex.31: 4), and they may devise iniquity (Ezek.11:2; Mic.2:1).

I would say, in the light of the above, that the image of God was in man's soul, not bodily resemblance, though the greatness of man's self radiated through his wonderful physical structure. Man was, though finite, God-like in holiness and righteousness and in knowledge, and in knowledge he is far above the highest creature of the animal kingdom. Of holiness and righteousness the animals know nothing whatever. Already redeemed men and women are created in Christ Jesus for good works, works of which they were incapable in their unregenerated state (Rom.3:10-12; Eph.2:10), while as yet they are mortal, as regards their bodies. Paul also says that the woman is the glory of the man; here he leaves out the word "image." She was made for man to be his helper and companion. Paul speaks of two women who proved helpers to him in labouring with him in the gospel (Phil.4:2,3).

1 Cor.11:8,9,10

Paul in verse 8 states what was true of man and woman at their creation, that the man is not of (Gk. ek, out of) the woman, but the woman of (Gk. ek, out of) the man; she was builded by God from a rib which He took from man's side. Man was not created for, or on account of, or for the sake of, the woman, but the woman for, on account of, the man. She was to be his helpmeet to answer to his need in every respect, spiritually, mentally and physically. Because of this the woman ought to have a token of authority (that is, that she is under the man's authority) on her head, something to indicate that she is under the man. This last statement about the angels has given rise to many ideas and conjectures, both ancient and modern.

One of the most sensuous is based on the fabulous interpretation of the sons of God (fallen angels) taking wives of the daughters of men (Gen.6:1,2,4), and the danger of unveiled women falling a prey to bad angels. Angels, good and bad, are not sexed, hence there is neither marrying nor giving in marriage among them (Matt.22:30). This is one of the wildest of the interpretations. Let us ask the question, What is the parallel between the woman and angels? Is it not this, that in the woman's case, the manner of the woman's creation shows her place is one of subjection, and in consequence there must be a token of that subjection manifest on her head? Similarly, the angels are in subjection to their Head, and with them also there is a token of that subjection manifest. What is that token is not revealed. This seems to me to be the simplest explanation of a somewhat obscure statement.

1 Cor.11:11,12

"In the Lord," describes a state of subjection to the Lord's authority, hence verse 11 does not describe the married state, that each man and woman must be married persons. Such a consideration would destroy much that the apostle wrote in chapter 7: The Fellowship expressed in the churches of God is one of men and women, not men only or women only. The Scriptures contemplate men and women being together under the Lord's authority. As the woman is of (Gk. ek, out of) the man in creation, so is the man by (Gk. dia, by means of), that is, born of the woman in the procreation of the human species. As man and woman are interdependent on one another, both sexes are of, that is, dependent on, God who is the Creator of each.

1 Cor.11:13,14,15

The woman is to be veiled or have her head covered when she prays with others in God's assembly, but besides this her hair is given her for a covering. The covering of her hair is expressed by a different word from her being veiled. The hair and the veil are two entirely different things. In these verses Paul deals with the length of hair of the sexes. Long hair is a dishonour to the man, and long hair is the glory of the woman. This is what even nature teaches, Paul says. Women should not lightly cast away their long hair, which is their glory, and seek to ape the man. God would have a clear distinction between the sexes, in hair, in head covering or no head covering, and in dress. Such is God's ordinance and should be observed. Betrousered women are just as unseemly as a man in petticoats.

1 Cor.11:16

There are few things that have caused more trouble than that of subjection. Here Paul deals with subjection in relation to man and woman in the church. Woman's hair also has been a matter of trouble and has caused some measure of disquiet in the churches. The fashion of the world affects those who do not set their mind on things above, where Christ is. Nature teaches women to have long hair. The word nature (Gk. phusis) has been described as "a native feeling of decorum, a native sense of propriety." Long hair in Israel was a mark of beauty, as is seen in beautiful but wicked Absalom (2 Sam.14:26), and it was a mark of holy men, as in the case of the Nazirite (Num.6:5). One could understand that what Paul says in this part about the hair might cause some dissension among the Jewish believers, if not among the Gentiles. But Paul says of any one who seemed to be contentious about the things of which he wrote, that no such custom existed, nor did it exist in the churches of God. There could be no disputing about the teaching he had just given on the matter of subjection and the sign of it, and also on the matter of the hair. This was given with apostolic authority.

1 Cor.11:17,18

The charge that Paul refers to is that from verses 2-16, which deals with matters affecting the conduct of men and women when gathered in church. Paul did not praise them, for their coming together was not for the better but for the worse. The reason for his saying this was, that he had heard that schisms, which mean splits or rents, existed among them. He said that he partly believed it. See 1 Cor.1:10.

1 Cor.11:19

Strange as this statement may seem, that there must be heresies among the saints (Gk. hairesis, a choice or option), such heresies or choosings by factious schismatics were to the end that those who were approved by God would be made manifest among them. Alas, there have been, and I think, will ever be the schismatics, the choosers and troublers in assembly life, whose choice and conduct ever reveal their inward state, and the distinction between them and the approved becomes clearly manifest. Paul warned the Romans against such as were causing divisions, and occasions of stumbling, contrary to the doctrine which they had learned as disciples, and they were to turn away from them (Rom.16:17). Such as were proven heretics were to be rejected after a first and second admonition (Tit.3:10).

1 Cor.11:20,21,22

Their coming together was not "into one place" as in the AV/KJV; the Greek words rendered "together" in RV are epi to auto, which mean "upon the same thing." See Acts 1:15; 2:1,44,47, also 1 Cor.14:23, where the words are used. The manner in which they sought to carry out the Lord's supper was entirely improper. The word in the Greek for "Lord's" here is not a possessive noun, but Kuriakos, an adjective. It is used here to describe the supper, and is used in Rev.1:10 to describe the day. It is never used elsewhere in the New Testament. Instead of eating the Lord's supper, they each ate before other his own supper, one was hungry and another drunken. They failed to observe two things, the necessary unity of action in doing this together and not individually, and they were making the Lord's Remembrance a matter of appetite, a matter of the stomach and not of the heart. If it was their appetite that required consideration, then they had houses to eat and to drink in.

Despite the fact that their condition and conduct were to be deplored, we learn in these verses where the Lord's Remembrance is to be observed, even in and by a church of God, and nowhere else. This cannot be over-emphasized. Many things we learn through the failures of others. There was nothing against the saints in Corinth satisfying their appetite in their own homes before they came together for the Lord's Remembrance. But how many there are who professedly come together, to do what the Lord commanded His disciples to do on the night of His betrayal, with an empty stomach, as though they could eat Christ with the mouth and digest Him in the stomach! How gross are the thoughts of men as deceived by the Devil! The Lord's supper is a remembrance by those who know Christ as their Saviour by personal faith in Him, and is not a means of salvation from hell. Only persons who are already saved should keep His Remembrance.

1 Cor.11:23,24

Paul goes over again what he had previously delivered to the Corinthians, and which he had received directly from the Lord, not from the apostles which were before him. In the night of His betrayal, we know from the Gospels, the Lord took bread or a loaf (Gk. artos, a loaf or a thin cake of bread). The Holy Spirit uses artos, the common Greek word for bread, not azumos (negative a and zume, leaven), unleavened, or unleavened cakes or bread. Had the Lord intended the breaking of the bread to be observed with unleavened bread, clear instructions would have been given as to this doctrine in so important a matter as that of His Remembrance, and especially so for Gentiles who were not accustomed to the restrictions regarding leaven as the Jews were.

But the Lord does not make it a matter of doctrine, simply specifying that it must be kept with a loaf of bread. Paul indicates four things which the Lord did with the bread. (1) He took bread, that is, He took the loaf into His hands. He did not elevate it as in the Romish mass, in what is called the elevation of the host. (2) He blessed ("it" in the AV/KJV is in italics showing that there is no equivalent Greek word for "it"; "it" should not be in the text); blessed has the same meaning as giving thanks. See Lk.22:19, and also here in Corinthians. (3) He broke the bread, symbolic act of His death. (4) He gave the broken bread to His disciples, symbol of the fact that He was about to give Himself for them. Did the Lord perform an act of transubstantiation when He said the words, "This is My body, which is given for you"? No, He certainly did not.

If He had changed the substance of the bread in His hands into His corporeal, and literal body which was born of the Virgin Mary, then at that time He had two bodies, one in which He was living, which was born of the Virgin, and which was soon to hang upon the cross, and another in His hands. It is the most utter folly to think that there were two bodies born of the Virgin. If the Lord did not change the bread which the disciples ate into His literal body, then all the priests of Rome that ever lived or are living now certainly cannot change one morsel of the numberless wafers of the Romish communions into the literal flesh of the Lord. Where is the Lord's body now? It is in heaven, and in it He is seated at the right hand of God, so that it, in no sense, is on Romish altars in many lands. What the Lord did He enjoined upon His disciples to do, and that unto a remembrance of Him, not to remember Him. To remember Him is an act of the memory and this we do daily and many, many times a day, but what He instituted was a remembrance in an act by the assembled church. It is done not unto salvation, but unto a remembrance.

1 Cor.11:25,26

As the Lord had done with the loaf, so also did He with the cup. He took the cup in His hands; He gave thanks; He poured it out; and He gave it to the disciples and told them all to drink of it (Matt.26:27; Lk.22:20). The cup was the cup of the New Covenant, which New Covenant found its base in His blood, that is His blood shed on the cross. It is the blood of the Eternal Covenant (Heb.13:20). It is the blood by which the New Covenant is ratified, and in consequence is now in operation with all its benefits and blessings to those that believe. "For where a testament (the same Greek word as for covenant) is, there must of necessity be the death of him that made it. For a testament is of force where there hath been death: for doth it ever avail while he that made it liveth? Wherefore even the first covenant hath not been dedicated without blood" (Heb.9:16-18).

The shedding of the Lord's blood ("and apart from the shedding of blood there is no remission") is symbolized in the pouring of the cup. Note that Luke says that the cup was poured out for them. The words of Lk.22:20 rendered literally are, "This the cup ... which for you is poured out, (is) the New Covenant in My blood." "New Covenant in My blood" describes what the cup symbolizes. It is clear that the Lord who instituted His own Remembrance did not Himself partake of the bread or the cup. We must be clear that what we are to do is what He told His disciples to do, firstly, to do as He had done, in taking, giving thanks, breaking the bread (and pouring the cup), and giving to the disciples, and also, secondly, partaking jointly of the symbols. We must not divorce these two things. Some divide the breaking of the bread into two (1) the doing of what the Lord did, and (2) the eating and drinking. The words in Corinthians are read as though they said, that "by" the eating and the drinking we proclaim the Lord's death till He come.

Note, that they say no such thing. The words are "as often as," not "by." Note that the previous words say, "This do, as oft as ye drink it, in remembrance of Me." Here we have the Remembrance associated with the drinking of the cup. What shows the Lord's death more vividly than the breaking of the loaf and the pouring of the cup? Nothing, in the whole service of the Lord's Remembrance. The breaking of the bread is to go on each Lord's day (the first day of the week) until He comes. There are (1) the day on which the breaking of the bread is to be kept, the Lord's day; (2) the way in which it is to be kept, as the Lord instituted it; (3) the people who are to keep it, God's gathered-together saints; and (4) the place where it is to be kept, in the church of God. Such principles of truth are similar to those in connection with the keeping of the Passover.

1 Cor.11:27,28,29

The death of the Lord was the result of the breaking of His body and the shedding of His blood, symbolized in the breaking of the loaf and the pouring (or shedding) of the cup. The person who partakes of the loaf and the cup unworthily, in an improper manner, shall be as those who are indifferent to the Lord's atoning sufferings, who are guilty of the body and blood of the Lord, as truly as those who nailed Him to the tree. Indeed, greater light brings greater guilt. Unworthiness at the breaking of the bread will bring its due punishment, as we see that it did in the later verses in this chapter. We eat and drink judgement to ourselves if we discern not the body. Though the word in verse 29 (AV/KJV) "Lord's" ("of the Lord") is deemed by some not to be part of the original there can be no doubt that the body is the Lord's own body, seen in the symbol in the loaf, and not His Body the Church, nor yet the body of assembled saints. Each person is to prove himself or herself and so to eat.

1 Cor.11:30,31,32

Here we have the judgement indicated, in verse 29, in persons eating and drinking judgement to themselves. Many of the Corinthians were suffering from the Lord's chastening hand in consequence of their carnal disorders at the breaking of the bread. Though saints may be guilty of the body and blood of the Lord, they will not be condemned with the world for this. The Lord may judge them and in consequence they may be weak and sickly in body, or they may even be put to sleep and sent away off the earth as being unworthy of a place in God's assembly. Personal discernment as to our state is a very necessary thing in connection with the Lord's Remembrance. Where wrong exists this should be dealt with and confessed and forgiven. God will in due time deal with the world for slaying His Son.

1 Cor.11:33,34

Here he returns to their disorder (verse 21), of one being hungry and another drunken, and each one taking before other his own supper. The Lord's Remembrance being a collective remembrance by the church, in coming together they were to wait one for another and not be acting independently of each other. Again, the eating of the Lord's supper was not a matter of appetite, it was a thing for the heart, its memory and affections. If any one was hungry he was to eat at home. This indicates, that in the apostle's thoughts and those of the Spirit of God, there was no thought that the saints should come together with empty stomachs to partake of the bread and wine of the Lord's Remembrance, as ritualists erroneously do. As for the rest in connection with any disorders, Paul proposed to wait to put these right when he came to Corinth.

COMMENTARY ON 1 CORINTHIANS 12

1 Cor.12:1,2,3

There can be no spiritual gifts or spirituals in any one apart from a person being first of all indwelt by the Holy Spirit. In the past of their life the Gentile believers in the church in Corinth were led away unto dumb idols, in the blindness and darkness of idolatrous deception, a deception which was of the devil and demons. In contrast to the dumb idols, the Spirit of God was One who spoke, and no one speaking in the Spirit of God could, far less would, say that Jesus was anathema, that is accursed. Likewise, no one can say that Jesus is Lord but in the Holy Spirit. Such a confession that Jesus, the Man of Nazareth, is Lord, required the Spirit's enlightenment, and also the acknowledgement in that confession that he who confessed this was in subjection to Him as His bondservant.

The Lord said, "Why call ye Me, Lord, Lord, and do not the things which I say?" (Lk.6:46). To say that Jesus is Lord is not to be mere liptalk. In this sincere confession was the beginning of all spiritual gifts and manifestations of the Spirit to profit withal. We must recognise that many of the gifts mentioned afterwards in this chapter belonged to the miraculous period at the beginning of this dispensation when there was no New Testament in existence, and when men needed to be assured that the testimony borne by the apostles and others was truly of God. When the testimony was confirmed by miraculous evidence and the books of the New Testament were written, the miraculous gifts disappeared, for the Lord had confirmed the word by the signs that followed (Mk.16:20; Heb.2:3,4).

1 Cor.12:4,5,6

Though there is but one Spirit, there were diversities of gifts through the Spirit dividing to each one severally as He would (verse 11). There were diversities of ministries (Gk. diakonia, the work of a deacon, who is one who serves or ministers to others), and the same Lord, who gives to each of His servants his part in His service for which the Spirit has gifted him. There are diversities of workings (Gk. energema, an operation or working) but the same God who operates all things in all persons. Thus we have the Trinity in action: the Sprit imparting the various gifts to each as He will; the Lord giving to each in His service the service for which he is suited according to the gift of the Spirit, and the Father the Director who empowers the operations in all persons.

1 Cor.12:7,8

The manifestation of the Spirit is how the Spirit chooses to act in each one to whom He has been pleased to impart a gift. The object of the gift is unto the profit of the saints. It should make the receiver of the gift humble, rather than that the gift should exalt him, and through pride fall a prey to that which is the condemnation of the Devil, even pride. To one is given the word of wisdom, and to another the word of knowledge. Knowledge and wisdom are not synonymous. Wisdom is the right use of knowledge. "The tongue of the wise uttereth knowledge aright" (Prov.15:2). It is said that "knowledge directs a man what is to be done, and what is not to be done; but wisdom directs him how to do things duly, conveniently and fitly." Again it is said, "We affirm with confidence that Sophia (wisdom) is never in Scripture ascribed to other than God or good men, except in an ironical sense ... there can be no wisdom disjoined from goodness." Such gifts of the Spirit may still be with us for the help and guidance of the saints.

1 Cor.12:9,10

Salvation is the gift, in Eph.2:8, and not faith. Here faith was a gift given to certain saints, in the Spirit. Though some may have strong faith now, it is doubtful whether this gift is still given. We know that all saints have obtained a like precious faith (2 Pet.1:1), though all may not put it to use. We know too that God has dealt to each a measure of faith (Rom.12:3), but what is in verse 9 is faith of an outstanding kind which some had in excess of others. To another was given gifts of healings. This was not the gift of healing, such as to heal any or everyone that applies as in advertised healing campaigns now-a-days. It is gifts of healings according to God's will according to the peculiarity of each case in the diverse sicknesses from which the afflicted suffered. The knowledge of God's will in each case was essential. Today, if no benefit results from the would-be curer, the blame is put upon the poor patient. To another was given the workings or operations of miraculous powers. To another was given prophecy; it was very necessary when saints had no New Testament that there should be men who were in touch with God to deliver His message to His saints. To another was given the discerning of spirits; the ability to prove the spirits (1 Jn 4:1). Today we have the New Testament Scriptures by which we can prove the spirits which speak by the mouths of men, for as truly as God's doctrine must be sounded forth, so truly are there the doctrines of demons (1 Tim.4:1).

In the apostle's time the New Testament was in the course of being delivered in its several parts from time to time. To another was given the gift of tongues (languages), and to another the interpretation of tongues. The gift of miraculously speaking a language and knowing what was said by the speaker himself was not given beyond the miraculous period at the beginning of this dispensation, and this applies also to the interpretation of tongues. More will be said on this matter when we reach chapter 14: The gifts of wisdom and knowledge may still be with us. The gift of faith as here is doubtful. But there can be no doubt whatever that the other gifts, those of healings, prophecy (as regards foretelling future events, and giving special messages from God) have ceased. Now such as may prophesy (1 Cor.14:3,4) give their message from the written word. Discerning of spirits, diverse kinds of tongues and the interpretation of tongues, belong to the miraculous period, as we have said, which was at the beginning of the dispensation.

1 Cor.12:11

Here we have another proof of the personality of the Spirit. He has a will, which is not true of a thing or an influence. In giving His gifts He divides to each one severally as He will. He is not influenced by external causes, but acts according to His sovereign will. The giving of gifts is His work.

1 Cor.12:12,13

The human body is an organic unity which has many members, and all the members form one body; so also, we are told, is Christ. Christ here is not the person of Christ, but Christ the Head and His members. This Body of the Head and the members is formed by the Lord baptizing each believer in one Spirit, the Holy Spirit, into the one Body, and at that time each member was made to drink of the one Spirit. It should be noted that it is not that we are baptized by the Spirit, as in the AV/KJV It is clearly seen from Matt.3:11 that the Lord is the Baptizer, even as Jn the Baptist said, "I indeed baptize you with (En, in) water ... He shall baptize you with (En, in) the Holy Spirit. This work began at Pentecost (Acts 2), even as the Lord said, in Acts 1:5, "For Jn indeed baptized with (or in) water; but ye shall be baptized with (En, in) the Holy Spirit not many days hence."

It should be carefully noted by such as speak, professedly, in tongues, that whereas all the believers in the church in Corinth were baptized in the Holy Spirit, yet they did not all speak with tongues. A slight consideration of verses 9,10, 29,30 of this chapter shows that they did not all speak with tongues. It is rank heresy to teach that all believers in this dispensation are not baptized in the Holy Spirit, but only such as speak with tongues. If only such as speak with tongues are baptized in the Holy Spirit, then the Church which is Christ's Body is a very small thing indeed. It is a pity that any should cheat themselves and others in this matter of membership of Christ's Body. In the members of the Body there are no racial or social distinctions, all believers of every race, and colour, bondmen and freemen, men and women, are all one in Christ Jesus, members of Christ and of one another.

1 Cor.12:14,15,16,17,18

Paul follows on with what he said in verse 12 about the human body illustrating the Body of Christ. He repeats what he said in verse 12 about the body being not one member, but many; hence one member cannot say that it is not of the body because it is not another member, or has not the gift of another member. Each member has its own gift and its own function to perform, and each member performs its function not for itself alone, but for the good of the whole. If we could imagine members of the human body, moved by pride or self- seeking, performing their functions for themselves or, shall we say, going on strike and refusing to work, into what a hopeless state the body would develop. But this never happens, though, alas, such a state of things exists in organized society, and even among believers the most inconsistent state of things obtains.

Thank God, such a state of things does not penetrate into the Body of Christ. God has placed the members of the human body as it pleased Him. If the members of the human body could be moved about by the whims of fashion and fancy, what weird and wonderful human beings would be seen moving about! But God does not allow man to change the location of his members or their peculiar gifts. As true as God has placed the members in the human body as it has pleased Him, so truly has He set the members in the Body of Christ.

1 Cor.12:19,20,21,22

There is nothing useless in the human body, nor is there anything unnecessary. It is God's work and therefore a perfect whole, each member and part having its own peculiar work to do. Paul imagines the members talking to one another on the need the one has for the other. If believers understood more the lesson taught them by their own bodies, they would see the need that they have for one another. It is not a matter of tolerating one another, but they need one another, as much as the eye needs the ear, and the hand the foot. We can live without a hand or a foot or an eye or an ear, but we cannot live so well as when we have them. A glass eye is a poor substitute for a real one, and a wooden leg for the natural one. Even the feeble parts of the human body are necessary.

1 Cor.12:23,24

The human body has what we think to be parts that are less honourable, yet "upon these," says Paul, "we bestow more abundant honour." The comely parts have no need of being made more comely. Even so there are members of the Body of Christ whose gifts are of the lesser sort, and whose path is more lowly than that of more highly endowed members. Hence the lesson would be that upon these lowly folks more attention should be paid than upon those whose gift brings them more into prominence. God has tempered the body together (tempered, Gk. sugkerannumi, to mingle together, to blend with, to join in such a manner as that one part or ingredient may qualify another).

1 Cor.12:25,26

God tempered the body together that there should be no schism (division or rent) in the body. The human body is one organic whole, all the members being perfectly set in their places by God, and so perfectly adjusted as mutually to serve each other and serve the whole body. Consequently the members have the same care for one another. This is a most elementary lesson, yet a very profound one, when the parable of the human body is applied to the Body of Christ. It is impossible for one part of the human body to be divided from the rest and left uncared for. This would mean death for that part. Thus when one member suffers all the members suffer with it. Its pain is their pain. We all understand this from experience.

Also, when one member is honoured, such as, say, the putting an engagement ring on a lady's finger, all the other members of her body rejoice with the honour done to that finger, for it is done to the whole. The arguments of Paul in this whole passage are to emphasize the truth of the organic unity of the members of Christ who are joined to Him in one Body.

1 Cor.12:27

What is Paul's meaning here? Is he saying that the saints in the church of God in Corinth are the Body of Christ to the exclusion of the saints in all the other churches of God elsewhere? Certainly he is not! Again, is it necessary to be in a church of God to be in the Body of Christ? Certainly it is not! Why? Because a believer is baptized in the Holy Spirit into the Body of Christ the moment he is born again, as see what happened to Cornelius and his company in Acts 10:44,45: It says, "While Peter yet spake these words, the Holy Spirit fell on all them which heard the word. And they of the circumcision which believed were amazed, as many as came with Peter, because that on the Gentiles also was poured out the gift of the Holy Spirit." This is the normal way in which the Holy Spirit is given throughout the dispensation, as see Jn 7:37-39: No one can be in a church of God who is not baptized in water (Matt.28:18-20; Acts 2:41,42), and that takes place some time after Christ has baptized the believer in one Spirit into the one Body; then it is some little time after that before the person is added together with those who are already in a church of God.

Verse 27 above states exactly the same truth as Rom.12:5, which says, "So we, who are many, are one Body in Christ, and severally members one of another." Indeed there is no definite article in verse 27 above, so the apostle is not speaking objectively as in our English versions, "Ye are the Body of Christ," but subjectively, "Ye are Body of Christ." The saints in Corinth were characteristically Body of Christ, with all the saints in Christ elsewhere, that is, they were "one Body in Christ," and each one severally was a member thereof, and had been from the time when they were born again.

Let me state my understanding as clearly as I can; the Body of Christ is not composed of groups of saints, i.e. local churches, those churches in their aggregate forming the Body of Christ. The Body of Christ is not composed of churches of God in one Fellowship, but is ever seen as composed of members, and a saint is a member from the time of regeneration, not from the time of addition to a church of God. Then it may be asked, Why did Paul write to the saints in Corinth as to their character as Body of Christ? It was that they might in their assembly life, as dwelling together in unity, exhibit what God had made each one of them, even a member of Christ, and thus being members of Christ their Head, and members one of another, they should have the same care for one another as he had just showed that the members in the human body have for one another.

Also, that as the members of the human body are fitted with peculiar gifts to serve the body, even so were the members of the Body of Christ endowed by the Spirit to serve each other and the whole Body as far as their gift extended. Let it be clearly stated that all may read and learn and be clear as to the Faith in regard to church truth, that whereas the Church which is Christ's Body is ever one, there were many churches of God in the time of the New Testament. Many such churches, but one house of God, and many members, but one Body. Again it is perhaps necessary to say that the house of God is not the Body of Christ.

1 Cor.12:28

While in verses 4-11 we have different gifts given to different members of Christ, we have here in verse 28 the gifted persons or the members themselves set in the Church which is Christ's Body. The Church here is not a local church or church of God. See also Eph.4:7-11, where the gifts are the men who were given by the ascended Head for the perfecting of the saints, unto the work of ministering, unto the edifying of the Body of Christ. The first in order of the members with diverse gifts that God set in the Church were the apostles, the chief ministers of Christ in this dispensation. The apostles have never been repeated, though there have been false apostles in ancient times and also in times more modern. Second to these were the prophets, to whom the gift of prophecy was given, as in verse 10: These also have not been repeated. They, with the apostles, laid the foundation of which Christ Jesus is the Chief Corner Stone (Eph.2:20). Those who would build for eternity must build on this foundation.

Then there were the teachers, men who were able to expound the Scriptures, and instruct the saints and so perfect them in their understanding of God's will. These men have been continued, as well also the evangelists and the pastors, as in Eph.4:11: Then we have miracles or powers, gifts of healings, and diverse kinds of tongues; these have not been continued; they belong, as we have before said, to the miraculous period at the beginning of the dispensation. We have also helps and governments; these we judge still continue with us. Helps are persons who give aid or render assistance, and governments (Gk. kubernesis, a governor or director, from kubernetes, a pilot or helmsman) are such as were elders or overseers, men who stood before the saints and took the lead and were over them in the Lord. See 1 Thess.5:12; Heb.13:7,17; 1 Tim.5:17: Such men are with us still. Diverse kinds of tongues belonged to the miraculous period, and are not with us today.

1 Cor.12:29,30,31

The answers to the seven questions of the apostle is, No, in each case. All saints were not apostles, and also all did not speak with tongues, but all were baptized in the Holy Spirit and so became members of Christ's Body (verse 13). Thus we see the folly of those who teach that speaking with tongues is an evidence of baptism in the Spirit. Indeed, speaking with tongues was a sign in the apostle's time, not to such as believed, but to the unbelieving (1 Cor.14:22), but now, when persons babble in making sounds which they cannot understand it is taken as a sign that they have been baptized in the Spirit. But more anon on this subject when we come to chapter 14: The saints were to desire earnestly the greater gifts, and a still more excellent way of conduct of the members of the Body Paul was about to write about, as is given in chapter 13.

COMMENTARY ON 1 CORINTHIANS 13

1 Cor.13:1

To speak in tongues of men means to speak in men's languages, and similarly in regard to the angels. Paul alludes here to the eloquence of men and of angels whatever language may be spoken, and great is the power of eloquence to sway men. If such oratory is not directed by the love of the speaker, then it is but as sounding brass and a clanging cymbal, probably two kinds of cymbals.

1 Cor.13:2

If one had the gift of prophecy, having been introduced into the secrets of the divine mind and knew all that is possible for man to know, and had so great faith as to remove mountains, yet had not love, all these other great endowments were nothing. Love then is the spring of all things, of service both to God and man. Love is the fulfilment of the law, and upon the two great commandments, "Thou shalt love the Lord thy God ... and thy neighbour as thyself," hang the whole law and the prophets. In addition to what the law said, the Lord gave to His disciples a new commandment, that they should love one another as He had loved them (Jn 13:34; 1 Jn 2:7,8). Love is the nature of the Divine Being, for God is love, and he that loveth not knoweth not God. Love makes heaven, heaven, and hatred will make hell, hell; in the former the saints will be glorified, and in the latter sinners will be punished, where men will hate their very being and will wish to cease to be, but cannot.

1 Cor.13:3

If for any other reason than love, acts of philanthropy (which means love of mankind) are unprofitable to the giver, however profitable they may be to the receiver. The motive of giving to feed the poor must be love, not to add to the glory of the giver or to join in the upsurge of a popular movement. Also, as for the martyr, who for some other reason than love, gives his body to be burned, it will profit him nothing. There have been those who for church or state have suffered martyrdom, but not for love's sake; that will be unprofitable for them.

1 Cor.13:4

Love suffers long and bears in patience, and it is kind. Kindness means to give what will be serviceable and useful to another with a gentle beneficence. Love knows neither wicked jealousy nor envy. It does not go in for display, and is not an arrogant boaster. It is not puffed up or inflated with pride.

1 Cor.13:5

Love makes gentlemen and gentlewomen; it does not encourage one to behave in an unbecoming manner. The Christian who is actuated by love is modest and retiring. Love seeketh not its own. "Let no man seek his own, but each his neighbour's good" (chapter 10:24). Love is not provoked, that is, not quickly excited to indignation, and if provoked, the Christian is not to let the sun go down upon his provocation (Eph.4:26). Love reckons not evil nor imputes evil to the person who has wrought the evil.

1 Cor.13:6

Love cannot rejoice in wrongdoing; it ever aligns itself with the truth and rejoices in it. Those in whom love dwells cannot be companions of such as are given to acts of unrighteousness and lying. Those who would walk according to love must leave those whose principles are not principles of righteousness, if they would walk in and rejoice with the truth.

1 Cor.13:7

Love beareth (Gk. stego, to cover, conceal, also to keep silence, to endure) all things. "Love covereth a multitude of sins" (1 Pet.4: 8). It believeth all things; it is not suspicious of what another says, yet it proves all things (1 Thess.5:21). Love hopeth all things; "Hope putteth not to shame; because the love of God hath been shed abroad in our hearts through the Holy Spirit which was given unto us" (Rom.5:5). Thus love is the well-spring of hope. We may even hope for better things for such as are entangled in evil. The Christian should be essentially a hopeful, not a hopeless man. Love endureth all things, even as the blessed William Tyndale, when being martyred, sought mercy for Henry VIII, when he cried, "Lord, open the eyes of the king of England." What glorious endurance of the martyred host! God's love in their hearts was the cause of it.

1 Cor.13:8

Love never faileth (Gk. pipto, to fall), as other things will; it knows no end. Prophecies (Gk. propheteia, a message delivered under the influence of the Spirit) were to be done away, that is, made useless. Tongues were to cease; this means the miraculous speaking with tongues, not that speaking in a language would ever cease, for that is one of the great gifts of God to all men. Knowledge, which means knowledge in part, is also (Gk. katargeo) made useless. But how is this knowledge made useless? It becomes useless because of the coming of that which is perfect. At the same time speaking with tongues ceased.

The question that arises is, What is "that which is perfect"? Is it a perfect revelation or a perfect state? I would take it that it is a perfect revelation, which makes useless that which is fragmentary and dim. In the advance of human knowledge primitive instruments and weapons of ancient peoples were rendered useless by the advance of knowledge. It is of course to be acknowledged at once that in the Old Testament the New Testament lies concealed. Things which were not understood by

God's saints of the past are now made plain by the Spirit's light in the New Testament Scriptures.

1 Cor.13:9,10

When does that which is perfect come? The answer to this question may fall into one of two views, (1) that it came when the Faith had been delivered to the saints (Jud.3), or (2) at the coming of the Lord in the future. Mr. Alford makes the following comment: "Chrysostom, al., understand the two first futures (Katarg., – done away – Paus., – cease -), of the time when, the faith being everywhere dispersed, these gifts should be no longer needed. But unquestionably the time alluded to is that of the coming of the Lord." This note sets the matter in clear perspective. I am disposed to the view of Chrysostom, that in verses 8,9,10, the full revelation of the Faith rendered prophecy (and also part knowledge) unnecessary, and that the speaking with tongues ceased as a sign to men of the divine character of the Faith which was proclaimed by the apostles and others. There is no doubt that a state of perfection is in view in the verses which follow, which will be revealed in the coming of the Lord.

1 Cor.13:11,12,13

These are the days of our childhood. The Lord called His apostles "babes" (Matt.11:25). They were babes to Him who is the Eternal Word and the Wisdom of God. The divine Scriptures are perfect. Inspiration is a divine and perfect work, but man's knowledge of what is inspired must ever be relative. It is ours to do as the prophets did of old, to search them diligently (1 Pet.1:10-12), to see new beauties and to gain greater riches. But in many things we see as in a glass, darkly. The reasons for this may be manifold; first of all, there is the fact that we weak and finite creatures are dealing with things divine and eternal; then lack of education and of the original languages; lack of spirituality and of being in harmony with the Spirit who is the Author of the Scriptures; failure to read the word and to spend time in prayerful meditation therein; worldliness and the lust for material enjoyment; and other things which may occur to the reader's mind, all combine to keep the believer in the condition of a child, perhaps during the most of his lifetime.

"Now I know (Gk. ginosko, to learn, to know) in part," says Paul, "but then shall I know (Gk. epiginosko, to know fully) even as also I have been known" (fully known). It will be a Rev.to know ourselves fully as the Lord has known us. There must, in the very nature of things, in realms eternal, be much that will never be fully known by us, but in comparison with our present childhood days, we shall know what cannot be known now, save, as the apostle says, we see things darkly. Now in contrast to what must in its nature cease and be done away, there are the things that abide, faith, hope and love. These shall abide when time shall be no more, and the greatest of these is love.

COMMENTARY ON 1 CORINTHIANS 14

1 Cor.14:1

After his digression to write at length on love, the greatest treatise on the subject in the Scriptures, Paul takes up again the matter of spiritual gifts. Whilst they are to pursue love, they are to desire earnestly (Gk. zeloo, to be zealous, to have strong affection toward) spirituals or spiritual gifts or manifestations, but rather that they might prophesy. Prophesying here is giving a message from God in the Spirit for the edification of the church, not of necessity foretelling future events. Greek propheteuo, to prophesy, is derived from pro, before, and phemi, to say or speak. It signifies forthtelling as well as foretelling.

1 Cor.14:2,3,4

A tongue was a language spoken by some race of people. "Speaketh" is from the Greek word Laleo, to utter words, to talk. The Greeks made a difference between lego and laleo, the former "signifying to speak with meditation and prudence," and the latter "to speak imprudently and without consideration." The person who spoke in a tongue unknown to the church spoke in his spirit what were mysteries to them, for no one understood him. In contrast to this, the one who prophesied, speaking in the language known to the church, spoke unto the edification, the comfort and the consolation of the church, three excellent effects of the divine message he delivered. It was of the nature of Isaiah's message of old: "Comfort ye, comfort ye My people, saith your God," and he spoke of the coming of Jn the Baptist and of the Lord (Isa.40:1-11). "He that speaketh in a tongue edifieth himself."

Some say that the person who spoke in a tongue did not know what he was saying. If this had been so, how was it possible for any one to edify himself if he did not know what he was saying? One can no more edify himself if he does not know what he himself is saying, than he could edify any one else who did not know what he was saying. In fact, he would be a barbarian to himself. See verse 11: In contrast, the one who prophesied in the language known to the church edified the church. There is no mystery about what Paul is saying; it is simple and straightforward instruction, though many have mystified many others with their interpretations.

1 Cor.14:5

He that prophesied was greater, Paul said, than he that spoke with tongues, except the tongues were interpreted; then and only then was it profitable. The object in all speaking was that the church might be edified.

1 Cor.14:6,7,8

Paul further deals with the unprofitableness of speaking with tongues, unless what is said is known by the hearers. Revelation is necessary to prophesying, and knowledge to teaching. Prophesying is the result of something which God has revealed, which is conveyed in a message to whomsoever sent. Teaching is the giving instruction to others by those who have themselves, by patient study, been instructed by the word. Then Paul turns to things without life which are made to give a variety of sounds, the pipe, harp and trumpet, and if these do not give a distinction of sounds which are understood by the hearers, what is the profit in the sounds? They are but a jumble of noises.

1 Cor.14:9

Here are a few potent words calculated to correct the abuse of the gift of tongues, and they should be heeded by such as profess to speak with tongues today. A tongue or language is the vehicle of thought, and unless it is this, to babble with words is no better than the prattle of a child. Speech in public should be clear and understandable, otherwise the speaker is wasting his own time and that of his hearers. It is as Paul truly says, speaking into the air. The speaker might as well be addressing himself to a herd of cows in a field.

1 Cor.14:10,11,12

The world is full of voices as never in any age before; some voices, and these are the most, are vanity, and some convey matters of great importance. But if the meaning or power of the voice is unknown, then the speaker and hearer are barbarians (Gk. barbaros, a foreigner who speaks a different language) to each other. The Corinthians were zealous of spirits (or spirit manifestations). In the past they had been accustomed to the idol and to demons (1 Cor.10:20), and with the obscure manifestations of the workings of demons, and now, it seemed to the be the case, that they were more taken up with the obscure utterances of speaking with tongues than with the edifying of the church. The edifying of the church was the proper objective of public speaking. There is, we believe, in the modern babbling which passes current as speaking with tongues in the spiritual sense, much of the working of demons causing people to ejaculate sounds of which they do not know the meaning.

1 Cor.14:13,14,15

The person who spoke in a tongue was to pray that he might interpret what he said in a language unknown to the church. Verse 28 shows that if there was no one present who could interpret then the speaker in a tongue was to be silent in the church and he was to speak to himself and to God. If a person should pray in a language unknown to the church, then his spirit prayed, but, though he understood what he himself was saying, his understanding was unfruitful, that is, unfruitful in his hearers, for they knew not what he said. Paul said that he himself would pray with the spirit, and he would pray with the understanding also;

that is, he would pray in such a way as that those who had heard him would understand what he said. Likewise he would sing with the spirit, and with the understanding also. This was just common sense, and requires no spiritual attainment to understand the fitness of what he said.

1 Cor.14:16,17

If a person should bless, that is, give thanks, with the spirit, but without the understanding, that is, not being understood in what he says, how was he who did not understand the language that was being spoken, filling what is called the place of the unlearned or illiterate, to say the Amen at the giving of thanks, seeing he did not know what was said? The place of the unlearned does not mean a person who is unsaved or one who is given a seat assigned to such as are not in the Fellowship; it just means a person who is unlearned, who does not know the language in which the person is praying. The one who prays may give thanks well, but the other is not edified, seeing he is ignorant as to what is said.

1 Cor.14:18,19

Paul here states again in effect that he did not despise speaking with tongues, for he spoke in tongues more than all the Corinthians. But in church, when saints were gathered together, he would rather speak five words with his understanding, that his understanding might be conveyed to others, than ten thousand words in a tongue which no one understood. His object was always to speak in an understandable way so as to instruct others. The wisdom in this course cannot be questioned.

1 Cor.14:20

Here Paul sums up his argument on the matter of speaking to the edification of the church. In this display of speaking with tongues, they evinced a great deal of childishness. He exhorted them to be full-grown in mind, but babes who had not yet learned the evil of malice.

1 Cor.14:21,22

The law in its widest application means the entire Old Testament. This quotation from the law is from Isa.28:11,12: In Jn 10:34 we have a quotation from the law, from Ps.82:6: Similarly in Jn 15:25 we have a quotation from Ps.35:19: In Acts 2 God spoke in tongues to the Jewish people, that is, in foreign languages, and though a few thousand repented the Jewish nation would not hear. This sign was ineffectual upon the Jewish people – "not even thus will they hear Me, saith the Lord." "Tongues are for a sign," says Paul, "not to them that believe, but to the unbelieving." Those who today profess to speak with tongues take their speaking with tongues as a sign that they have been baptized in the Holy Spirit, so that in their case it is not a sign to the unbelieving, but to those that believe, the reverse of what Paul says. Modern speaking with tongues is a satanic deception. Prophesying is a sign, not to the unbelieving, but to them that believe, for it is unto edification and comfort and consolation.

1 Cor.14:23,24,25

Paul speaks here of the whole church being assembled together (not "into one place," as in the AV/KJV, but together, Gk. epi to auto, "upon the same thing"; see 1 Cor.11:20). If all spoke with tongues and men who were illiterate and unbelieving came in, Paul asks, "Will they not say ye are mad?" Truly, it would seem to them that it was so. But if all prophesied, one by one (verse 31), the messages from God would reach the unbeliever's heart, and he would be convicted or searched into by all. The secrets of his heart, Paul says, would be manifest, and falling down on his face he would worship God, declaring that God was among them. This must have been a remarkable evidence of the work of the Spirit in the man contemplated in the passage. Such conviction is rare in our times.

1 Cor.14:26

What was this coming together of the church for which Paul gives instruction as to godly order? Can it be doubted that it was when the church was in church assembled on the first day of the week for the breaking of the bread? Each one hath a psalm, that is, a song of praise; a teaching, that is, an exposition of some part of the word; hath a revelation, he exercises his gift of prophecy in delivering God's message; hath a tongue, that is, he speaks in a language not known to the church; hath an interpretation, that is, what is said in a foreign language is interpreted into the language spoken by those in the church. No doubt the coming together for the breaking of bread was a longer gathering than that which obtains at the breaking of the bread today. In Acts 20:7 it stretched out until midnight. Possibly, too, those who took part on such occasions took less time to say what they had to say than some do today. The prime matter was, that all things were to be done unto edifying.

1 Cor.14:27,28

Such as spoke in a tongue were to be limited to two, or three at the most, and that in turn. But if there was no interpreter present the speaker in a tongue was to keep silence in the church. It seems to me that this called for some previous arrangement between the speaker in a tongue and an interpreter. It does not seem fitting, according to Paul's instructions, that a speaker in a tongue should begin and continue to speak in a tongue, expecting there might be someone present who could interpret, only to find that there was not. If there was no interpreter present, then the speaker was to keep silence and to speak to himself and to God. We ask, If the speaker in a tongue did not know what he said, according to modern tongue-speaking, how could he speak to himself? It would be folly to think of him attempting to speak to himself if he did not know what he was saying. It would be mere babbling to attempt to speak to God, if he did not know what he said. That he knew what he said is evident, but he might not be able to interpret what he said into the language spoken by the church.

1 Cor.14:29,30

As with the speakers in tongues, so with the prophets, they were to speak by two or three, and the rest of the church were to discern or discriminate as to what was said. But if a revelation was made to another of the prophets sitting by, the first was to keep silence. Paul's instructions enjoin not only the utmost freedom in those who were fitted to take part in the proceedings, but also manifest subjection of the one to the other. The Spirit had liberty in such an assembly to use whom He would for the edification of the saints.

1 Cor.14:31,32,33

"Ye all can prophesy," quite evidently means, all to whom God had revealed something for the edification of the saints. The object of prophesying was that all might learn, and all might be comforted, exhorted or encouraged. Neither speaking with tongues nor prophesying were ecstatic utterances which took the control of a person's spirit out of his own hands, for the spirits of the prophets were subject to the prophets. A prophet could keep silence if he willed to do so, and speak when and as he thought fit. For several people to be babbling at the same time is not of God for God is not the Author of confusion or disorder, but of peace, and peace was to find its place in all the churches of the saints. The churches of the saints were similar to the churches of Christ (Rom.16:16). Nowhere in the New Testament do we read of "a church of Christ" or "a church of the saints." We judge that such churches were different companies of the saints who met in different parts of the city, forming the one church of God in the city.

1 Cor.14:34,35,36

Having given inspired instructions concerning the behaviour of men in the gathering together of the church, Paul now turns to that of women. His instructions concerning the women are simple and clear. "Let the women keep silence in the churches: for it is not permitted unto them to speak." Many have tried to circumvent these words by casting aspersions on the apostle, such as, that he was not a married man, and that it is only Paul's opinion, and such like. But let verse 37 be read and it will be seen that Paul says that what he wrote was "the commandment of the Lord." We live in times when the word of God has little weight on the consciences of the many. God's order is disrupted both by men and mannish women. The sexes are set in opposition to each other, instead of it being seen that they are complementary to each other in a common race, each suited to its own functions and place in the economy of things as God ordained them. The women's place is one of subjection, but not of inferiority.

According to the law in Israel there were no female priests or Levites, no female elders or rabbis. Women were not allowed to speak or ask questions publicly in the church; asking questions was to be in the domestic sphere. As it was in the law, so in New Testament times, there were no female apostles or prophets, no female evangelists, pastors or teachers. No woman is ever recorded as speaking in tongues or interpreting tongues. Nothing could be stronger on the point than the apostle's words, "It is shameful for a woman to speak in the church." For women to go contrary to this, they could go contrary to anything. The church of God in Corinth was not at liberty to institute a new custom of their own, which, had it been tolerated, would have amounted to, in effect, that the word of God went forth from them, or that it had come unto them alone. They had to be subject to the same teaching as obtained elsewhere, which was the teaching of the apostles (Acts 2: 42), which was the teaching of the Lord and of God the Father (Jn 7:16,17).

1 Cor.14:37,38

Whatever a man in the Corinthian church might think of himself, whether as a prophet or spiritual, he was to take knowledge of the inspired character of this epistle, stretching back from the commandment with reference to women, prophets and speakers with tongues, to chapter 1, in which epistle many disorders in that church are dealt with. The inspired character of the epistle has never at any time been in doubt. "But if any man is ignorant," said Paul, "let him be ignorant." If he were ignorant and preferred his own opinions, then he, with all others of like kind, was hopeless, and to seek to recover him from his stupidity would have been unprofitable; he must be disregarded.

1 Cor.14:39,40

Paul exhorts the brethren to prophesy and not to forbid speaking with tongues, but all was to be done decently, in a comely manner, and according to order or arrangement.

COMMENTARY ON 1 CORINTHIANS 15

1 Cor.15:1,2

In this chapter, which deals with the truth of resurrection, that is, the bodily resurrection of the saints in particular, which apparently some in the church in Corinth were denying, Paul goes back over the ground to the gospel which he preached among them, and he says, "Wherein also ye stand (perfect tense, which describes a past event, the effect of which remains), by which also ye are saved (present tense)." "Are saved" is rendered by many in a continuous sense, as "are being saved" (Alford, Ellicott, Young, Englishman's Greek New Testament, Conybeare and Howson), as showing, I judge, that salvation is proceeding. Salvation from hell is not a matter of continuation or of final perseverance; the salvation of the sinner from hell by grace through faith is plainly and clearly stated in Eph.2:5,8,9, and that salvation is eternal salvation.

The matter in doubt with the Cor.is in the words, "except ye believed in vain" (Gk. eike, without cause), that is, that theirs was a faith to no purpose, which would be true, if they had believed in a Christ who had not been raised from the dead. We see no need whatever to depart from the RV and AV/KJV rendering, "the gospel ... by which also ye are saved." It is present tense, as is Eph.2:5,8,9, "By grace are ye saved" (AV/KJV We have the present tense joined to the perfect participle here). "If ye hold fast," at first sight seems to encourage the thought that they were being saved if they held fast. This we judge is not the meaning of the passage. Paul having said that the Corinthians had received the gospel, that they stood fast in it, and were saved by it, could not immediately thereafter say that they were saved conditionally, if they held fast the gospel. This would imply the falling-away doctrine root and branch.

"Hold fast" is the Greek word katecho, to hold fast or retain, and the AV/KJV with a fine sense of what Paul is saying renders the passage as follows, "By which also ye are saved, if ye keep in memory what I preached unto you, unless ye have believed in vain. For I delivered unto you first of all that which I also received, how that Christ died ... was buried ... and that He rose again the third day." Paul is questioning whether they retained in their memory the gospel which he preached, which was concerning the death, burial and resurrection of the Lord. The Greek conjunction ei here is not casting a doubt, but is used in his argument, as he does frequently in his writings, as for instance in this chapter; "If Christ is preached" (verse 12); "If there is no resurrection of the dead" (verse 13); "If Christ hath not been raised" (verse 14); see also verses 16, 17, 19, 29, 32: In none of these, where the same conjunction ei is used, are the matters of which he speaks in doubt. We reject the thought of salvation from hell being a continuous thing, and also that the believer can endanger such salvation by failing to hold fast.

1 Cor.15:3,4

Here is the essence of the gospel. It is concerning Christ who died for our sins, and was buried, and was raised on the third day, and such cardinal features of the gospel are according to the Scriptures – that is, the Scriptures of the Old Testament, though abundantly declared by the Scriptures of the New. Such were the facts about which the apostle questioned the Corinthians. All his arguments which follow rest upon the death and resurrection of the Lord, and if He be not raised from the dead, what then? Mankind as a whole is lost, all hope is gone! Many scriptures tell of His death, Ps.22, 69; Isa.53, and many, many others. Isa.53:9 tells of His burial. Ps.16:10 tells of His resurrection, and that it would be on the third day like Jonah the prophet (Matt.12:39,40). The experience of Jonah is not the only fact of Scripture which foretold the Lord's resurrection; His resurrection was according to the Scriptures.

1 Cor.15:5,6,7,8

Paul asserts that the Scriptures said that the Lord would rise on the third day, and now he cites certain of His appearances after He rose from the dead. No woman who saw the Lord in resurrection is among the citations. Cephas (Peter) is the first in the list. The appearance of the Lord to him is mentioned in Lk.24:34: Then He appeared to the twelve (Jn 20:19-29). Thomas was not with the rest on the evening of the resurrection when the Lord appeared, but he was present the next first day of the week, eight days after, both first days of the week included. Then He appeared to above five hundred brethren at one time, some of whom had fallen asleep by the time Paul wrote to the Corinthians, but the greater part were alive and could have borne witness to the resurrection. Then He appeared to James, possibly the Lord's brother (Gal.1:19), who at the time of the Lord's appearance to him may have been appointed an apostle.

Last of all, the Lord appeared to Paul, as unto one born out of due time. (Gk. ektroma, an abortion). He appeared to him on the road to Damascus and at later times (Acts 9:3-7; 22:17-21; 1 Cor.9:1). As to Paul describing himself as one born out of due time, or the abortion among the apostles, this definition will cause a great difficulty if we adhere to the usually accepted idea in the word, that it always means a premature birth, hence, if applied here in this sense, it would mean that Paul was made an apostle before the time that the others were called apostles. The Greek word does not help us beyond giving the meaning as an abortion. Parkhurst says that in the two passages of the LXX, Job 3:16, and Eccles.6:3, it answers to a Hebrew word which means "to fall" or "fall away." In both these passages the reference is to an "untimely birth." It seems that all that can be said about the word is that Paul viewed his call to the apostleship as untimely, not at the same time as the rest, that is, when the twelve became apostles, without thinking that he became an apostle before them.

1 Cor.15:9,10,11

Paul viewed himself as the chief of sinners (1 Tim.1:15), the last of the apostles, and less than the least of all saints (Eph.3:8). He said that he was not meet to be an apostle, because he persecuted the church of God which was in Jerusalem (Acts 8:1-3); he made havoc of it (Gal.1:13). But God's grace which was bestowed upon him was not found vain, empty, fruitless, for he laboured more abundantly than the rest of the apostles. Yet he did not take credit for this to himself; he said that it was to the grace of God which was with him that the credit was due. But whether it was he or the other apostles that heralded the gospel, "so we preached", said he, "and so ye believed".

1 Cor.15:12,13,14

The "if" here is not the "if" of doubt, but the "if" of an argument. There was no doubt that Paul had preached a crucified and risen Christ, and if so, how were some of the Corinthians saying that there is no resurrection of the dead? Taking them on their own ground, that is, as some said, there was no resurrection, then neither was Christ raised. Hence it followed, that Paul's preaching was vain, for a dead Christ could save no one, and their faith also was void and fruitless.

1 Cor.15:15,16,17

Following on, Paul says that he and his fellow-apostles were false witnesses of God, if Christ be not raised, for His resurrection was, according to God, a main part of their message. For if the dead are not raised, then neither hath Christ been raised, and if this was so, then their faith was vain (Gk. mataios, groundless), and they were yet in their sins.

1 Cor.15:18,19

Alas, if it were so, those who had fallen asleep in Christ, who had been preached as raised from the dead, have perished, gone to perdition. Assuming that Christ had not been raised, then those who had suffered much for His sake, the apostles and others, were of all men most to be pitied, having given up the pleasures of the present life for what was after all a delusion. Thus Paul like a skilful advocate makes his points in the case with great precision and telling effect. If there is no resurrection of the dead, (1) neither hath Christ been raised, (2) our preaching is vain, (3) your faith is vain, (4) we are found false witnesses of God, (5) ye are yet in your sins, (6) they that have fallen asleep in Christ have perished, and (7) we are of all men most pitiable.

1 Cor.15:20,21,22

Christ hath been raised from (Gk. ek, out of) the dead. He is the firstfruits of them that are asleep, that is, He is the firstfruits of the redeemed who sleep in the dust (Dan.12:2). No scripture speaks of the sleep of the soul, that is, that the disembodied person is in an unconscious state. See Lk.16:19-31; 20:37,38; Rev.6:9-11; 7:9-17: Both the righteous and the wicked are in consciousness, the one in conscious comfort, and the other in conscious suffering. The Lord did not fall asleep, He died; but saints fall asleep in Christ (verse 18) and fall asleep through Jesus (1 Thess.4:14). Through man (Adam) came death, and through Man (Christ raised from the dead) came also the resurrection of the dead. "In (en, as denoting the cause) Adam all die," that is, Adam was the cause of death; "So also in (en, as denoting the cause) Christ shall all be made alive." This should not be read as though it said, "so also all in Christ shall be made alive." "All" is as "all inclusive in Christ" as "all is in Adam." As Adam is the cause of death to all men, so Christ is the cause of resurrection of all men, not simply of the redeemed, for there shall be a resurrection of the just and the unjust (Acts 24:15).

1 Cor.15:23,24

Each will be raised in his own order (Gk. tagma, anything placed in order, series, hence used of a body of troops drawn up in military order). Christ is the firstfruits. The next to rise is not the Virgin Mary, who, the Roman Catholics say, has been raised from the dead and has gone to heaven in bodily form (this is untrue): the next to rise are the Lord's own who have been bought with His precious blood, amongst whom will be the Virgin Mary. These will rise in their own order, not all together. The first to rise will be the saints who compose the Church which is Christ's Body, as we learn later from this chapter and from 1 Thess.4:13-18: The Old Testament saints and others will be raised at the Lord's return to earth (Dan.12:1,2; Rev.11:15-18; 20:4-6). The infant dead will also be raised. "At His coming" (Gk. parousia, presence) includes, I judge, the Parousia for His saints of the Church, and the Parousia of the Son of Man (Matt.24:3,27,37, 39).

"Then cometh the end" must not be understood to mean that the end comes immediately after the coming of the Lord for His own. There are over a thousand years between the coming of the Son of Man and "the end." The Lord reigns with His saints for a thousand years, and after that there is the judgement of the Great White Throne (Rev.20:6,11-15). After this judgement the Lord shall deliver up the kingdom to God even the Father, having abolished all rule and authority and power contrary to God. The Lord will hand back the kingdom to the Father who committed all authority into His hands and all judgement also (Matt.28:18; 11: 27; Jn 3:35; 5:22,23,27, etc., 13:3).

1 Cor.15:25,26

Although the Lord has even now all authority in heaven and on earth, and He is Lord of both the living and the dead, He must reign manifestly till He has put all His enemies under His feet. The last enemy that shall be abolished is death, which with Hades (Hell) will be cast into the lake of fire (Rev.20:14).

1 Cor.15:27,28

God put all things under the feet of His incarnate Son; gave to Him all authority in heaven and on earth, but the Godhead is outside the authority of the Son. We have a shadow of this in Joseph in Egypt to whom Pharaoh said, "Forasmuch as God hath shewed thee all this, there is none so discreet and wise as thou: thou shalt be over my house, and according unto thy word shall all my people be ruled: only in the throne will I be greater than thou. And Pharaoh said unto Joseph, See, I have set thee over all the land of Egypt" (Gen.41:39-41). When the Son has carried out the will of God who subjected all to Him and has put all His enemies beneath His feet (Ps.2; Ps.8; Phil.2:9-11; Rev.2:26,27,etc.), then shall the Son be subjected to Him who subjected all things to Him, and God, Father, Son, and Holy Spirit, shall be all in all, when the Son shall have carried through the work of redemption and dealt with all His enemies, casting them into the lake that burneth with fire and brimstone.

The time which we may call an emergency, when the Son in his mediatorial work shall bring peace into the realm of God, shall come to an end. The subjection of the Son to the Father does not mean that the Son is inferior to the Father, for subjection does not imply inferiority. Many persons are subject to others to whom they are by no means inferior. Though the Son is equal in essence and nature to the Father in His Godhead, yet the Son is subject to the Father.

1 Cor.15:29,30

Notice the pronoun "they" in verse 29; "What shall they do," not "we do." In contrast, note "we" in verse 30: "Why do we also stand," etc. No such practice is found in the Scriptures as persons being baptized for (Gk. huper, on behalf of) the dead (persons). It was, according to Ellicott, a practice of certain outside the Fellowship in the apostle's time. Possibly such thought in the case of their friends who died without leaving any testimony that they had been saved, of saved persons who had not been baptized, that baptism by proxy would be available and bring blessing to their dead friends. Some may say, How ridiculous! But how much more ridiculous was it than for men to sprinkle infants (calling it baptism), thinking that some good accrues to the unconscious child. Yet this passes current daily.

The apostle shows how futile was this act of being baptized for the dead, if the dead were not raised, for baptism signifies death and resurrection. Let it be said again that the practice was not a scriptural one. Then the apostle asks, in the light of the view of certain that there is no resurrection, why should he and others who suffered so much stand in jeopardy every hour. Such a course would be folly, if there were no resurrection.

1 Cor.15:31,32

Paul said, "I die daily," which is similar to what he writes in 2 Cor.4:10, "Always bearing about in the body the dying of Jesus, that the life also of Jesus may be manifested in our body." Daily dying means daily living in resurrection life and power. He utters a protest or affirmation in what he calls "your boasting (or glorying) which I have in Christ Jesus before God, that they were the fruit of his work, but now, alas, the foundation on which his work rested, the resurrection, was being denied by some. What profit was there in his sufferings, if after the manner of men he fought with the beasts at Ephesus, if the dead are not raised?

No doubt Paul is alluding to what took place at Ephesus through the rioting of Demetrius and his fellow-silversmiths, as recorded in Acts 19:23-41: If there is no resurrection, then Paul and the rest of his fellow-workers might have joined in the unrestrained dissoluteness of the then present life in which many found their pleasure. Indeed, we all may eat, drink and be merry, if when we die that is the end of human existence. Some thought so, and some, alas, still think so. It is nevertheless one of the foundational doctrines of Christ that the dead will be raised, and we all may heed the call to weeping and mourning, to a daily dying, rather than to feasting and levity (Isa.22:12-14).

1 Cor.15:33,34

If they had been in company with the Greeks, who scorned the fact of the resurrection (Acts 17:32), then they were not to allow themselves to be deceived, for such evil company would corrupt them, for people become like the company they keep. The Grecian idea of no resurrection seemed to have intoxicated them, and the apostle seeks to awake them from their intoxicated and deceptive slumbers. "Awake up righteously," he says, "and sin not." Some, alas, had no knowledge of God; they were ignorant of His ways, His plans and purposes, and not the least of His purposes was that the dead would be raised up. This, as Paul shows earlier in the chapter, involved the resurrection of Christ and every human being besides. If there is no resurrection of the dead, we may close our Bibles, but what have we left? Nothing, but to look into the future on the shore of time as into a black and stormy sea with no light to guide us, no hope in what lies beyond. This is not the outlook of the believer in the word of God.

1 Cor.15:35,36

Here we have propounded a question which has cropped up in the human mind and in discussions innumerable: "How are the dead raised? and with what manner of body do they come?" God has not gone into details of how the resurrection of the dead will be accomplished. He has spoken in general terms in many parts of Scripture, and has plainly shown that there will be a resurrection of the just and the unjust (Acts 24:15), also a spiritual body, a body so strong and enduring as to be able to bear an eternal weight of glory (2 Cor.4:17), whereas the present mortal body in a few years becomes spent. Paul draws a parallel between the human body placed in the grave and a seed sown in the earth. He says that what is sown is not quickened, except it die. The principle in both cases is death and quickening. Death does not mean for men anywhere in the Scriptures cessation of existence or of being; it means a change of existence. In contrast, life does not mean existence, for there are many things which exist which have not and never had life, as we speak of life and as it is spoken of in the Scriptures.

A change takes place in what is sown, death to the seed and a quickening resulting in a new plant, which is generally much more glorious in appearance than the seed that is sown. When this change takes place it is the end of the seed that was sown; at the same time there is a relationship between that which is sown and that which is quickened, the plant proceeds from the seed that is sown.

1 Cor.15:37,38

We must be careful in deductions which we may seek to make from what Paul is saying here. The body which is given to the seed is a body which is given to what was sown, and in parallel to the apostle's argument, the resurrection body of saints is a body which is given to the body which was sown, that is, buried, and not a body given to the soul, for the soul or person who died went to be with Christ at death and not to the grave. Paul's language is simple and clear, and if we accept what he says in the simplicity of faith then all will be well. The seed that was sown was a bare grain, not the body of the new plant. To the grain of wheat God gives the body of a wheat plant. To each kind of seed He gives a body of its own, hence the endless species and variety of plant-life. God's unfailing law in nature is, "after its kind" (Gen.1:11,21,24, 25). This is the statute of the Almighty Creator.

Evolution in its extreme form has tried to belie the Creator's words and works; yet the stream of life on this earth flows on like a mighty Amazon despite all the vagaries of human opinion as to the origin of species. Nature comes and goes, ceaseless as the tides, and man can change neither the one nor the other; both are regulated from heaven by the creative and sustaining word of God, and that word is that of Him who slept in a boat in a storm on the sea of Galilee, and then awoke and rebuked the wind and said to the sea, "Peace, be still," and there was a great calm. Such is He who by His almighty power will raise the dead.

1 Cor.15:39

Here is a head-on collision between the Scriptures and evolution. Beginning from the lowest form of life to the ascent of man, evolution would seek to describe a gradual evolving of one form of life from a previous one in a long well-nigh endless staircase of hundreds of millions of years, till life has reached the static state which we see around us. Cows were cows and jackdaws were jackdaws, bears were bears and men were men since I was a boy over three score and ten years ago. But we are told that we must not think in terms of 70 years, we must think in terms of 70 or more million years. David speaks of a lion and a bear in his time, and all the animals now on the earth with all humans are descendants of those which were in Noah's ark perhaps four millenniums and a half ago.

Let us hold to the true words of God as given us in Gen.1 and those of Paul in the above verse, and not be led away into men's dreamland of imaginary things. Gen.1 begins at the opposite end from Paul. First God makes the fish, then the birds, then the beasts, and last, and greatest of all, man, whom He made in His own image. There is no missing link between the species, for there was never any link to miss.

1 Cor.15:40,41,42

What is Paul telling us here? First, he is telling us that all flesh is not the same, and pointing out the differences between that of humans, beasts, birds and fishes, and then he is telling us of the different kinds of bodies, celestial and terrestrial, of the difference between the glory of the sun, moon and stars, and even that each star differs in glory from another. He is telling us that the resurrection of the dead is like this, that there will be a difference between resurrected saints in the body of glory which will be given to them. Most of us can see and understand the difference that exists between heavenly and earthly bodies, and between the glory of the sun and the moon, but most of us who have not studied the stars would not have known that there was a difference in glory in each of these. Thus it will be, that though each saint will be like the Lord when He comes for the Church, each saint will be different from the other, and with this difference will go identification and recognition.

If saints were exactly identical in the glory, and there was no recognition of the one from the other, heaven would be a strange place. If the sun and the moon shone with the same glory who could tell the one from the other? Then again, if we think of men on earth, what utter confusion would exist if all persons were exactly alike! But all human beings are different even to the finger prints.

1 Cor.15:42,43,44

As soon as the spirit and the soul (the person) leave the body, then corruption sets in, and it becomes necessary to do, as Abraham said to the children of Heth, "Give me a possession of a burying place with you, that I may bury my dead out of my sight" (Gen.23:4). Note the force of the words, "a burying place with you." Sarah's body and the bodies of the dead of the children of Heth went into the same mother earth. Some think that unique benefits are to be derived from being buried in consecrated ground and ground sprinkled with holy water, but the worms are in that ground as well as in any other. Who can deny that the body of the dead person is sown in corruption? but, blessed be God, it is as true that it will be raised in incorruption. It is sown in dishonour. How dishonourable it is to bury the body of a loved one upon which you have bestowed so much affection! But it will be raised in glory.

With man is the act of dishonour, with the Lord lies the act of glory. Christ is never shown in the Gospels as attending a burial, but He raised the dead. It is sown in weakness, who can doubt this? Man is never so weak as in death. "How are the mighty fallen!" said David when he heard of the death of Saul and Jonathan. "Imperious Caesar, dead and turned to clay, Might stop a hole to keep the wind away: Oh that that man who held the world in awe Should patch a wall!" But the bodies of saints which have been sown in weakness will be raised in power, in the strength of eternal youth. The body is sown a natural body (Gk. psuchikos, soulish, a body animated by the soul), as in verse 45: Adam was moulded out of the dust, and God breathed into his nostrils the breath of life, and he became a living soul (Gen.2:7). It will be raised a spiritual (Gk. pneumatikos) body.

Man will not be a spirit being or a spirit in the resurrection; he will have a spiritual body, not a natural body as at present. All things natural, such as marriage, birth, and all things which pertain to this life will pass away. Saints will then be in a scene of spiritual realities. But let me emphasize again that saints will have bodies in the resurrection, but they will be spiritual bodies. "Our pain shall then be over, We'll sin and sigh no more."

1 Cor.15:45,46

The first Adam became a living soul by the action of God in in-breathing the breath of life into his nostrils. The last Adam (not the second adam), who is the Lord raised from the dead, became a life-giving Spirit, to impart life to, or to make alive, the bodies of such as are dead, "For since by man came death, by Man came also the resurrection of the dead" (verse 21). The first body is natural (Gk. psuchikos); the second body is spiritual (Gk. pneumatikos).

1 Cor.15:47,48,49

Paul's words here are in perfect alignment with those of Moses, in Gen.2:7, 3:19: Moses says, "The LORD God formed man of the dust of the ground," and Paul says, "The first man is of the earth (Ge, the land as distinct from the sea), earthy (Gk. choikos, of dust)." Adam, we are told, was the first man; there were no humans before him; he is the head of mankind as having come from the dust of the earth. The second man, the Lord raised from the dead, really and truly a Man in resurrection, is of heaven. He is the Head of such as are heavenly, those who will have bodies like unto the body of His glory (Phil.3:21). Paul concludes his argument by saying, that as we have borne the image of the earthy (Gk. choikos, of dust), we are like to Adam in these earthy bodies, so shall we bear the image of the heavenly, we shall be like the Lord in bodily likeness.

1 Cor.15:50

Flesh and blood describes man in his natural state. Man must be born again, born of water and the Spirit, before he can see and enter the kingdom of God. The Lord in Jn 3 does not say that man enters the kingdom of God by the new birth, but that the new birth comes before his entrance thereinto. As natural man cannot inherit the kingdom of God, there being no relationship between him and that kingdom, even so corruption does not inherit incorruption. There is no relationship between corruption and incorruption. Indeed the two are diametrically opposed. Inheritance is based on relationship. Following this we have it explained how that which is corruptible shall put on incorruption, in other words, how that which is sown in corruption shall be raised in incorruption.

1 Cor.15:51,52

Paul reveals a secret, the secret being that we shall not all sleep, but we shall all be changed, both the living and the dead in Christ. "We" here are not simply the Corinthians with Paul and the saints then alive, but all the saints of this dispensation of grace down to the time of the Lord's coming. This fact is also made clear from 1 Thess.4:15-17, where we read of the living and the dead in Christ being caught up together – to meet the Lord in the air. The change in the bodies of saints, whether alive or dead, will take place in a moment (Gk. atomos, indivisible, an indivisible point of time. From this word the word "atom" is derived, a word so much used in this atomic age). This "moment" is called the twinkling of an eye. The change in the bodies of the living and dead in Christ takes place at the last trump (Gk. salpinx, may either be a trumpet or a trump, that is, the sound of a trumpet; Alford gives trumpet-blowing).

We may safely follow the AV/KJV and RV, both of which give "trump", the sound of a trumpet, not the trumpet itself. The following Greek word is a verb, salpino, which means "to sound a trumpet," which is rendered "the trumpet shall sound." Whether "the last trump" means the last of several trumpet blasts or whether it is the crescendo at the last of a trumpet blast is not clear. It may be something like the sounding of the trumpet when the LORD descended upon mount Sinai. It says that "the voice of the trumpet waxed louder and louder" (Ex.19:19). Whichever be the correct view, the change in the body condition of the saints takes place at the last trump. Trumpets are referred to, in Rev.8:2,6- 12; 9:1,13; 11:15-18, also in Matt.24:29-31, but these are trumpets which sound after the Church has been caught up to be with the Lord. The last trump is similar to "the trump of God," in 1 Thess.4:16.

1 Cor.15:53,54

"This corruptible" means the corruptible body of the saint who has fallen asleep; it must, it is imperative, put on incorruption or incorruptibility, and the mortal body of the living saint must put on immortality. This is not the soul or the person of the saint who has fallen asleep putting on incorruption and the living putting on immortality, but it is the corrupting body of the saint who has fallen asleep putting on incorruption, and the mortal body of the living saint putting on immortality. This is similar to what Paul says, in 2 Cor.5:1-4, where the apostle compares the mortal body to a tabernacle, and immortality to a house not made with hands, which at the Lord's coming shall clothe the mortal body of the living saint, and then that which is mortal shall be swallowed up of life.

When death takes place the saint is spoken of as naked, that is, he has left his earthly tabernacle, and in his case his corruptible body must put on incorruption. He too has a house not made with hands, eternal, in the heavens. The longing of the apostle, as well as of all the saints who have been enlightened as to the Lord's coming again, is that the Lord would come while they are yet alive, so that they should not be found naked. When the mortal puts on immortality, and the corruptible puts on incorruption, then shall come to pass the saying, which Paul quotes from Isa.25:8: "Death is swallowed up in victory." A victory is won in the bodies of saints, for corruption and mortality will resist what is contrary to their natures.

The change in the bodies of saints will be wrought by the Lord's power, "according to the working whereby He is able even to subject all things unto Himself" (Phil.3:21). The same power by which the Lord will put all His foes beneath His feet will be needed to deal with the powers of corruption and mortality in the bodies of His saints. Let us remember that mortal and immortal are words in the Scriptures which relate to the body and never to the soul or person, though men in their loose use of terms speak of "the immortal soul," a term never used in the Scriptures. This has led to entirely wrong ideas.

1 Cor.15:55,56,57

We have here a quotation from the LXX of Hos.13:14, though not exactly as given there. There seems little doubt that the RV is correct, giving "O death, where is thy victory," instead of "O Hades (grave, AV/KJV), where is thy victory?" In contrast to what was true in the past dispensation, prior to the death and resurrection of the Lord, when all the dead went to Hades or Sheol, the wicked to the place of fiery torment therein, and the righteous to the place therein called Paradise, the place of comfort and rest (Lk.16:19-31; 23:42,43), no saint in this dispensation goes to Hades. All saints in this dispensation of grace go to heaven at death to be with Christ which is very far better, and to be at home with the Lord (2 Cor.5:6-9; Phil.1:23). In their case death holds the body, but has no claim or hold upon the soul or person as Hades had in the past, prior to the crosswork of the Lord.

A complete and permanent victory will be won over death when the bodies of the saints are taken from its power. We are told that the sting of death is sin, and a fearful and deadly weapon it is! Then we are told that the power of sin is the law, for by the law came the knowledge of sin, and when the law entered sin became exceedingly sinful, and the law worketh wrath (Rom.3:20; Rom.4:15; Rom.7:13). Where there is no law there is no transgression. Paul, as he contemplates the glorious victory which will be wrought at the Lord's coming, bursts out in a note of thanksgiving, and says, "Thanks be to God, which giveth us the victory through our Lord Jesus Christ."

1 Cor.15:58

In the light of the glorious triumph which faith sees in front, saints are to be firm and immovable, not to yield ground one inch to the forces within and around themselves, but to be always abounding, ever increasing, in the Lord's work. Such labour is not vain or to no purpose in the Lord; it must be subject to His will, not as they or others may think that His work should be done. The day will come when saints and their work will stand together, for the worker will not be severed from his work.

COMMENTARY ON 1 CORINTHIANS 16

1 Cor.16:1,2

No wonder the poor, the widows and fatherless, were in a state of poverty in Jerusalem, for the Lord revealed the rapacious character of the rulers, when He described them as "they which devour widows' houses, and for a pretence make long prayers; these shall receive greater condemnation" (Mk.12:40; Lk.20:45-47). Jerusalem was ever a hotbed of trouble because of the sin and hypocrisy of the Jewish people. No wonder that poverty stalked the city among the poorer classes, whilst the rich Sadducees and Pharisees enjoyed their luxuries. To meet the poverty amongst the saints in Jerusalem, Paul encouraged collections to be made in the churches in Galatia, Macedonia and Achaia.

The saints were to lay by them in store (Gk. thesaurizo, to collect, to accumulate) each Lord's day as the Lord had prospered them (God's house is a storehouse – Mal.3:10 – and happy and blessed will they be who bring as they have prospered their gifts, as Israel was enjoined to bring the tithe, into the storehouse). This was to be done that no collections would require to be made when the apostle came. In the early chapters of the Acts we see the need of many, and the magnificent response on the part of those who were able to give. First they sold their goods, and then as the need continued they sold their houses and lands. "Not one of them said that aught of the things which he possessed was his own" (Acts 4:32). It is well to keep a light grip on what we have and not say that it is our own absolutely. There was never a community of goods for a community of people. If this had been the Lord's will for His people, that there should be a central purse out of which the need of all should be met, then the instructions given by Paul to the churches of the Gentiles were quite unnecessary.

1 Cor.16:3,4

When Paul wrote his second letter to the Corinthians, they had not even then attended to this matter of their contribution to the bounty for the poor in Jerusalem. He spoke highly of what the churches of Macedonia had done in giving, despite their poverty, indeed, he said that "their deep poverty abounded unto the riches of their liberality" (2 Cor.8:1-5). He called upon the Cor.to "complete the doing." The Corinthians were rich in words, but poor in works. He suggested that men should be sent to bear their bounty, and if he himself went they could go with him. From this we gather that Paul did not anticipate that their gift to the poor among the saints at Jerusalem would be a mere pittance.

1 Cor.16:5,6

We are told, in Acts 19:21,22, that Paul purposed in the spirit, that is, his spirit, to go from Ephesus through Macedonia and Achaia, and from thence to Jerusalem, and he sent Timothy and Erastus before him to Macedonia. Then followed the rioting of Demetrius and his fellow-craftsmen in Ephesus. After this uproar Paul took leave of the disciples "and departed for to go into Macedonia" (Acts 20:1), and from there he went on to Greece (verse 2). It would seem from 2 Cor.1:15-17,23, that prior to his purpose to go from Ephesus to Macedonia, he had thought to go from Ephesus to Corinth, probably by sea, and from there to go to Macedonia, and then back to Corinth, and from there to Judaea. He altered his plans of travel, as he says, "to spare you I forbare to come unto Corinth." It is evident from verse 8 that at the time of writing this epistle his purpose was to tarry at Ephesus until Pentecost.

The Lord's work there was going on apace, as we learn from Acts 19, until the rioting of Demetrius and his fellows. His words in verse 5, "for I do pass through Macedonia," do not mean that he was passing through Macedonia at that time, but that his purpose was to pass through Macedonia in his journey to Corinth. He hoped to winter in Corinth, and he spent three months in Greece, and though he intended to sail to Syria, he again had to alter his plans, because of a plot of the Jews, and he returned through Macedonia instead (Acts 20:3).

1 Cor.16:7,8,9

The events in Ephesus, when a great door and effectual was opened unto him, are recorded in Acts 19: Paul said also, that there were many adversaries. Acts 19:20 says, "So mightily grew the word of the Lord and prevailed." Alas, Satan's work of opposition was soon manifested in the efforts of Demetrius and his fellows to bring God's work to nought. What was the root cause of the rioting? – money, silver, covetousness, idolatry. This cancer overspreads the earth still.

1 Cor.16:10,11

The carnality and pride of the Corinthians on the one hand, and the youthfulness and perhaps a measure of timidity in Timothy (1 Tim. 4:12) on the other, caused Paul to strike a note of warning to the Corinthians. Timothy was to be with them without fear, for he, like Paul, wrought the work of the Lord. Timothy was no stranger in Corinth, as we learn from Acts 18:5: He was to be set forward on his journey in peace, perhaps to meet Paul as he came from Ephesus through Macedonia. The brethren that Paul refers to may be some of the mighty men of Acts 20:4:

1 Cor.16:12

Paul who directed the movements of many of the Lord's servants in those early days, shows here that he did not dominate them. He besought Apollos much to go to Corinth, but it was not the will of Apollos to go at that time, but he hoped to go later when the opportunity presented itself to him. This is a guide in making suggestions to the

Lord's servants regarding the Lord's work; the decision rests with the Lord's servant himself as he is led of the Spirit.

1 Cor.16:13,14

Paul exhorts them to vigilance, and that they should stand fast in the Faith, that is, the apostles' doctrine which Paul had delivered to them. They were to be brave and manly in the Lord's things and to be strong. Strength of character and of purpose is to be admired. All things were to be done in love, the true motive in all Christian action.

1 Cor.16:15,16

Here we have a devoted household, that of Stephanas, the firstfruits of Paul's work in Achaia. Epaenetus was the firstfruits of Asia unto Christ (Rom.16:5). In the light of this household who devoted or addicted themselves to the service of the saints, where are the household baptizers? It is said, in Acts 18:8, that "many of the Corinthians hearing believed, and were baptized," amongst whom undoubtedly was the household of Stephanas. What is true of this household of Stephanas is undoubtedly true of Lydia's household, and of the jailor's household, in Acts 16; there were no unconverted persons therein, or small children who had not reached the years of responsibility. Here Paul calls for due subjection to those who devotedly work and labour in the Lord's service. There was to be no carping criticism of the Lord's labourers, such a Korah and his company levelled against Moses in the past (Num.16).

1 Cor.16:17,18

I see no need for the alteration that Alford and others have suggested here, that "the want of you," as they render it, is "of your society." I judge that what Paul is referring to is what these three servants of God from Corinth brought to him, and was what the church in Corinth should have sent to the apostle, but failed to do so. The case is similar to what the church in Philippi sent to Paul by Epaphroditus (Phil.4:17-19), but with this difference, in the latter case it was the church in Philippi that sent the gift, and in the former it was these three good men who brought their gift, the church in Corinth having failed in this. They refreshed the apostle's spirit, even as they had been wont to do the spirits of the saints in the church in Corinth. They were to be acknowledged in the good work which they were doing.

1 Cor.16:19,20

We conclude that this epistle was written from Ephesus (see verse 8). We have already commented on the words, "I do pass through Macedonia," which shows Paul's intention, but is not equivalent to, "I am passing through Macedonia," as though he was journeying through Macedonia at the time of writing. From Ephesus he sends the salutation of the churches in the province of Asia, and also that of Aquila and Prisca, who were well known in Corinth, for they were there at the time of the planting of the church of God there (Acts 18:1-4), and they left Corinth with Paul and came to Ephesus (Acts 18:18,19) where he left them. Paul also sends the salutation of the church which met at (not in) the house of Aquila and Prisca in Ephesus. The brethren were to salute each other with a holy kiss, a mode of salutation in existence then. The custom of salutation now is to salute each other with a warm shake of the hand.

1 Cor.16:21,22,23,24

Paul sends his salutation with his own hand, but the epistle otherwise may have been written at his dictation by another, as was the epistle to the Romans which was written by Tertius (Rom.16:22). When all is finally summed up there will be but two classes, those that love the Lord and those that Love Him not (see Rom.8:28-30). Such as do not love the Lord will bring upon themselves the curse of God, and will have themselves to blame, for though God loved them so much as to give His Son, they would not receive His love in the Gift of His love. On the part of saints, love for the Lord differs greatly, and those love Him best who keep His commandments (Jn 14:21).

Whilst "Anathema" is a Greek word which means "accursed," "Maran atha" is Aramaic or Syriac. These words mean, "The (or our) Lord cometh," which may have been the salutation amongst Christians in the early days, until the thought faded out of His coming again. Here we have the well-known salutation of Paul, "The Grace of the Lord Jesus Christ be with you." He adds, "My love be with you all in Christ Jesus. Amen." Thus ends this magnificent epistle on church truth, on behaviour and discipline.

Did you love *Notes on the First Epistle to the Corinthians*? Then you should read *Needed Truth 1888-1988: A Centenary Review of Major Themes* by Hayes Press!

Needed Truth magazine celebrated its 100th anniversary in 1988. To commemorate, twelve authors were commissioned to write on twelve important topics that have featured prominently in the magazine over that century:

    CHAPTER ONE: THE INSPIRED WORD
    CHAPTER TWO: THE DEITY AND ETERNAL SONSHIP OF THE LORD JESUS CHRIST
    CHAPTER THREE: THE HOLY SPIRIT
    CHAPTER FOUR: ETERNAL SECURITY
    CHAPTER FIVE: BELIEVER'S BAPTISM
    CHAPTER SIX: THE BREAKING OF BREAD

CHAPTER SEVEN: FELLOWSHIP AND CHRISTIAN UNITY
CHAPTER EIGHT: THE CHURCHES OF GOD
CHAPTER NINE: THE HOUSE OF GOD
CHAPTER TEN: THE KINGDOM OF GOD
CHAPTER ELEVEN: THE COMING AGAIN OF THE LORD JESUS CHRIST
CHAPTER TWELVE: RESURRECTION AND ACCOUNTABILITY

Also by JOHN MILLER

New Testament Bible Commentary Series
Notes on the Epistle to the Romans
Notes on the Epistle to the Ephesians
Notes on the Epistle to the Galatians
Notes on the Epistle to the Philippians
Notes on the First Epistle to the Corinthians
Notes on the Epistles to the Thessalonians
Notes on the Epistle to the Colossians
Notes on the First Epistle to Timothy
Notes on the Second Epistle to the Corinthians
Notes on the Second Epistle to Timothy
Notes on the Epistle by James
Notes on the Epistles by Peter
Notes on the Epistle to the Hebrews
Notes on the Book of Revelation
Notes on the Epistles by John

Standalone
The Way of God
Notes on the First Epistle to the Corinthians

About the Publisher

Hayes Press (www.hayespress.org) is a registered charity in the United Kingdom, whose primary mission is to disseminate the Word of God, mainly through literature. It is one of the largest distributors of gospel tracts and leaflets in the United Kingdom, with over 100 titles and hundreds of thousands despatched annually. In addition to paperbacks and eBooks, Hayes Press also publishes Plus Eagles Wings, a fun and educational Bible magazine for children, and Golden Bells, a popular daily Bible reading calendar in wall or desk formats. Also available are over 100 Bibles in many different versions, shapes and sizes, Bible text posters and much more!

www.ingramcontent.com/pod-product-compliance
Lightning Source LLC
Chambersburg PA
CBHW031359040426
42444CB00005B/347